PUT YOUR MIND AT EASE

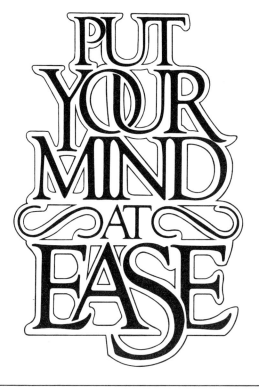

PUT YOUR MIND AT EASE

JOYCE HIFLER

ABINGDON PRESS
NASHVILLE

PUT YOUR MIND AT EASE

Copyright © 1983 by Abingdon Press

Illustrations by Leonardo M. Ferguson

Library of Congress Cataloging in Publication Data

HIFLER, JOYCE.
   Put your mind at ease.
   1. Meditations.   I. Title.
   BV4832.2.H5   1983   242   82-24316

ISBN 0-687-34929-X

MANUFACTURED BY THE PARTHENON PRESS AT
NASHVILLE, TENNESSEE, UNITED STATES OF AMERICA

The author wishes to acknowledge,
with special gratitude,
the newspaper editors through whom she reaches
millions of readers.
Many of the columns that appear daily across
the country as "Think on These Things" or
"Put Your Mind at Ease"
are included here.

To my friend and father-in-law
Martin I. Zofness
and
to my Charlie

. . . Your life will be brighter than noonday;
its darkness will be like the morning.
. . . You will have confidence, because
there is hope;
. . . You will be protected, and take
your rest in safety.
. . . You will lie down, and none
will make you afraid.
—JOB 11:17-19—

CONTENTS

PREFACE

It is the nature of the thinking, wondering, analytical, human being to have moments of elation—but also times of melancholy. Feeling dejected is not always the result of a problem, but can surface for no apparent reason— sometimes in our quietest moments.

Emotional stress is often blamed on a lack of mental or physical health, and sometimes there is a connection. In many instances, it is simply the need to express oneself in a better way—to reach farther and think more deeply than we have before. It does not mean we are lacking *anything*, but that we are capable of adding a new dimension to our lives. We may be at the door of having a greater capacity for accomplishing new and more exciting purposes. And when we do not recognize such development we feel heavy with the need for peace.

Outer conditions and their effect upon us will not decide our ultimate journey through life, but our inner attitudes and how we handle them will make that decision. But we can change whatever we want to change, leaving behind rigid ideas and bitter memories. Only then can we eagerly begin to enjoy life by weaving in the lovely colors and all the beautiful fibers that make our lives effective and serene.

ONE

SOMETHING OF A PERSONAL NATURE

*I will not let you go, except
that you bless me.*
—GENESIS 32:26—

ONE

I am my own holy mountain. . . . I am my own holy mountain at its highest prevailing point . . . when I am centered and poised . . . not in what I've been taught from the outside, but what I know from the inside . . . that I am not condemned except as I condemn me . . . that through the purest love that refines and molds me the wolf in me is quieted . . . and the lamb of me feeds alongside without fear of hurt.

I am the drop of water as complete within myself as any sea, filled with the hum of activity as any summer meadow, laced with merriment as the evening air full of children's laughter, and raised to the highest awareness of my own inner Universe.

I am the music of the spheres, the sound of the sweetest voice, the cry of the violin, and the cowbell on a crystal clear morning. I am the meadowlark, the whippoorwill, the high-pitched wailing of the coyote, and the owl's hoot at the blue hour.

I am the harmony that sweetens life and balances my threefold dependency on the One Presence promising that nothing shall hurt or destroy in all my holy mountain.

I am that inner person of everyone.

* * * *

There are bits of magic in the life of every person—little things that weave for us a fiber of living so strong we are sure it will bear us through the greatest pressures. These are the things that come to us in the quiet times—or sometimes in flashes of infinite understanding. They become priceless gems held close and protected from the heat of day and the critical eye. Then one day it seems the time for sharing—and wisdom ceases.

It ceases because there are so few persons with whom we can share, really share, the deep and amazing spirit that is the life of us. The spirit is a knowing, the God-life that heals and renews and holds calm the meaning of us as individuals. That which is so obviously important to one person may not create the same feeling in another. And though we want so much to share something special, if we do it too soon, the special meaning may very well vanish. But when that life of life has become a permanent part of our conscious existence, then nothing can destroy it, for it is like dipping into the sea for water—so quickly replenished.

*   *   *   *

Perfection in anything is a dream that continues to exist. It is that beautiful ephemeral vision we always hope to see, and even a hint of it is cause for glorification. Sometimes it seems our demands for it are far greater than our ability to recognize it.

There is always that search for the perfect love, the perfect friendship, the perfect job. But that kind of perfection is so vague, and we must have more than a mere desire to ever experience it.

We experience brief moments of flitting through something we sense as nearly perfect, but if we were to demand that the moment have lasting life, it could melt like an ice crystal in the sun.

On a day-to-day basis we can savor what we feel is perfect for even the swiftest instant—and then let it pass into longer times that may be a little less perfect, but oh so enduring. We can be sure that if there has been one perfect time, there can be others. It is enough to lift our expectations.

* * * *

Let me never take for granted a quiet lane alongside a field of ripe grain. Let me never forget to listen to the songs of a thousand birds—all with something to sing about.

Allow me to see the sky with its wisps of white cloud that turn rose and pink and gold in the evening glow. Let me feel the breezes gentle and filled with the scent of elderberry and grapevine.

Let me never wish for sunshine when the gentle rain is falling, or forget to appreciate the shade of the old oaks when the sun is at its strongest.

Let me appreciate all the fruits the earth yields and all the labor it takes to grow and harvest them. Let me know that this very moment is the life of life, and only I can live my own to the highest and best.

* * * *

Why is it that spring brings you to mind so vividly? Our friendship has lasted through all the seasons, and have we ever had to rely on such changes to make us remember? to recall the many laughing years? and yes, the tears? We've shared so many of the same feelings and felt the deep and enduring understanding.

Why must spring be the time of year so enhancing to our timeless friendship? What happens on this beautiful earth of ours to create such vibrations and bring out all the beauty?

It must be new hope, new life, a power yet unused . . . the power of love to transcend time and space and lost connections. It is the power that links us with the universe of all good, all peace, all that is ours by divine right.

It is the quiet partnership between friends.

* * * *

A team is a group in which each player, or worker, has a specific part to play. Wisely, they all know a lot about every part, but they work their own positions with precision and efficiency.

Every player cannot be captain, and every person cannot play quarterback. The part may be small, but if it is played with fairness and dignity, giving all, then it will be as important to the successful outcome as the biggest job in the organization.

The practical view of cooperation is vivid in John Dickinson's thought, "By uniting we stand; by dividing we fall." We are only as strong as the weakest and only as cooperative as the spirit in which we work.

People working together make things happen. There is such strength in numbers, power in hands and voices joined for a good purpose—or a bad one.

Most people have no real intention of getting caught supporting a bad cause. They simply get swept along with the tide, sometimes out of curiosity and sometimes out of ignorance. We have to know what we are lending our strength to and what ultimate purpose it serves.

When we can stand together with selfless concern for each other, accomplishment is unlimited. What the world does not need is more artificial grace or more poor-me attitudes.

We can make difficulty or we can make friends—with ourselves and with teammates—and opponents.

* * * *

It is a relief to know that every day we come in contact with people who put such confidence in us that we strive even harder to have something worthy to give. These are the persons who build human beings, and there is no job more delicate or more creative than giving someone the courage to do his best.

Building character and confidence in another person is a fragile operation. No two people ever respond in the same way. And there can be very little trial and error in deciding how to handle an individual. Where one person must be spurred, another needs free rein, and a third requires leading.

We are all human and we all have the need for approval, for a sense of accomplishment, but most of all, for attention. When we know someone cares, it makes all the difference in where we are going and how fast.

The harsh situations in life are often eased by one gentle considerate person, that special person who has such inner qualities of generosity and strength they never call attention to our inadequacies—though there may be many.

Francis de Sales once contemplated the strength of weakness, how nothing was as gentle as real strength. Our will is very strong in our decision to be weak, but in strength there is understanding and a gentleness that comes from the best part of us. It is a sweet gift of God.

To be that gentle, considerate person is a privilege not

everyone takes advantage of, or even finds very important, but with time we know its value and begin to see we must give to get.

*   *   *   *

There are special places in our lives that live on forever. Just entering those places in memory makes them live again. We feel the heat or the cold, catch the fragrance so familiar, the aroma of certain foods, or even hear a bit of a song.

There are too many reasons to count, too many feelings, for us ever to lose touch with some part of us that was then—and is now.

People are part of our memories, too—living within our thoughts and influencing our thinking like the wind that we feel but cannot see.

We are made up of many things, many experiences that we do not want to lose, but we also have the power to keep yesterday in its place and make the most of this day.

Yesterday was the foundation, but today is the house, and we're living there and keeping things in their proper order.

*   *   *   *

It is good to have someone to rely on . . . someone who doesn't calculate and keep score . . . someone who doesn't feel it a duty to criticize—as though the world needed another person handing out grade cards.

It is nice to know someone kind, someone who doesn't look at the world as terribly provincial, or feel grossly out of place in certain circles.

Much of what is wrong in the world is related to one

person's trying to fit another into a category, trying to label someone in order to make the person fit. Often in the process sensitivity is wounded and dignity is trampled, usually by those who are first to ask for kindness and reliability from others, but last to give it.

*   *   *   *

Alexander Pope once wrote of the American Indian,

> Lo, the poor Indian! whose untutor'd mind
> Sees God in clouds, or hears him in the wind.

It was a reverse sort of admiration for that human being who can so naturally see God in all of life, when it comes so hard for most.

Why is it so hard to be a natural believer? Why is it so difficult to keep faith sweet and simple and uncomplicated?

Why do we cloud every issue, every beautiful thing with so much that is rule and form and practice?

There is in every person's belief an uncluttered simplicity that speaks of a life-current between person and Creator. There is nothing dark or moody or fearsome, but only light and purity and freedom to talk from one's heart. It is a love that is beyond our normal understanding—a goodness we cannot destroy by tongue or hand, no matter how we may try.

*   *   *   *

How many times she called me to her side to share something beautiful—the glowing embers in a sunset, the call of a whippoorwill, or one of those rare moments when Venus draws near the new moon.

How many times she held my hand to comfort me

through hope and fear, birth and death, happiness and unhappiness.

How many times she taught me that no one is ever alone. We are always in the presence of the Father-God who loves us—no matter what might appear to frighten us.

How many times she said, "You can do it!" and how many times she refrained from saying, "You'll never make it!" And how many blessings I wish upon her—my mother!

* * * *

We make ourselves miserable a lot of the time by questioning why this or that has happened—what we did to deserve it. We debate why some people experience trouble and others slip through life in well-oiled grooves.

Why do some have to cry while others ignore the principles of living and suffer no apparent ill effects?

The nature of life is not always explainable. There is so much we do not know, so many things in disguise. Even in those whom we judge quickly as having no problems there are many dilemmas, many puzzles. Even they must wonder at the balance of things.

It is difficult to develop a talent or find a niche for oneself when there is no challenge. The pattern of events has proved more times than we care to recognize that we produce something worthwhile when we are pushed beyond our normal pace. Otherwise we tend to rest at a crucial point when we should be moving, and then we stall out completely.

It is our normal bent to watch what someone else is doing and forget our own responsibility. If other people are doing what they want to and get by, why shouldn't we? Maybe it is because we've been made aware of important areas others have not come to yet. Maybe we just don't know what someone else is dealing with.

When we take our attention away from the activities of other people we seem more able to forgive them for living the way they want to—and in forgiving we accomplish more, heal faster, and find a sense of self-worth. We align ourselves with some deeper, more spiritual perspective and live freely to enjoy our own reasons for being.

*   *   *   *

Can you see the wind? Can you see the fragrance of flowers floating on the breezes? Can you see thought or what it is that changes a tree from bare limbs and brown leaves to lush green?

Can you see love or joy or peace?

We can see only the results of these invisible things, but they exist. They are part of the most important substance of life.

Why, then, do we ever question the existence of the Creator, who set all these things in motion? The Very Highest is hardly known by mankind because we over-complicate and overload the simplest lines of communication. When we can see life in the lowliest ways we will have caught a vision higher than ordinary sight.

*   *   *   *

Sometimes to be young we first have to be old—to recognize that those things that once seemed so important have a place but are not the whole show.

Sometimes we have to feel the weight of problems in

order to push through those invisible walls that defy us to go anywhere.

Sometimes we have to lose the old self to find the new one—to put off the old habits to gain new ground, to know that it is not the years that teach us but our willingness to learn at any age.

Sometimes we get very tired and very disappointed, but to know the heights, we must rise above our emotions and taste the freshness of new heavens and a new earth.

*   *   *   *

There is something remarkable about a good husband or a good wife or those friends who stand so close to us that we take them for granted.

They are so much a part of us that we assume we know how they feel, what they think about, and that to share our lives is all they ever need.

By examining our own feelings we may suddenly realize they are not extensions of us, but individuals living a daily inner life that is unique and apart from our own.

They need as we need. And they are frequently more tactful than we are, sparing us the pain of our own faults and never correcting us because it would rock the boat.

We have often heard it said that when we have a good thing going we should leave it alone—except to cultivate it. When that happens to be a good partner, we need to give our protection and support in the hardest of times or, even more strenuous, in the best of times.

*   *   *   *

Like fingerprints and the leaves on the trees, like snowflakes and flower petals, we are each different from the other—and that is good.

Though there may be similarities and likenesses, there are always some little variations, some light differences that make us individuals.

It is not uncommon to see a person from another country or another part of our own country who seems like a fish out of water—different, so totally different that he stands out as unusual in speech, mannerisms, and even in thought.

Yet, like flowers, one is colorful, one has a lovely fragrance, one wilts easily, one is tremendously hardy, and one turns out to be a plain weed. It is the variation that makes the garden so exciting.

* * * *

Autumn sunrises are glorious shafts of gold that break under the trees to throw giant shadows across dew-drenched grass. The sight recalls the lines of an unknown poet.

> Lean thine arms awhile upon the windowsill of heaven and gaze upon thy Lord . . .
> and with that vision in thy heart turn strong to meet the day.

Sometimes a thing that seems so powerful breaks across our lives and throws giant shadows, and we are afraid. But it is only a turning point in the day, and we need to have enough vision to believe in greater things—to know that we are given strength to make new turns as we use our vision. The writer Lloyd Douglas said that when a man harbors any kind of fear it percolates through all his thinking. That is a luxury none of us can afford.

* * * *

Many summers ago I stood by you and said I would love and cherish and share with you the many experiences of life . . . and that in good times and bad we would hold each other's well-being in gentle and caring hands.

There has been nothing able to daunt that promise . . . and life in all its strange ways has served to strengthen and sweeten the day-to-day, moment-by-moment, realization that God is everywhere present with us.

No matter where I see you . . . standing in the sunlight, walking in the woods, laughing, or in deep concern . . . the dearness is always new, the respect is forever mutual, the joy is forever present . . . because you stood with me many summers ago and said you would share with me your marvelous life . . . and I love every solitary minute of it!

* * * *

Summertime, like most every other time, is cause for reflection. Maybe it's the heat that causes us to remember being barefoot on a country road thick with hot dust. And a creek flowing so slowly it takes forever for a curled leaf to float out of sight.

But things haven't changed all that much. The meadows are still full of wild petunias and horsemint and sunflowers. In early morning, a single dew drop on a holly leaf is a prism for sunlight, flashing brilliant red, then green, and finally blue.

To be aware of the present happenings is to recall sweetly much that has gone by—a hot summer day when a strawberry soda pulled from a container of icy water lasted only minutes, but its memory lasts for years. It doesn't have to be a life-rending occasion, but only a small treasure that lasts a lifetime.

* * * *

In times gone by porch-sitting was an art—the art of being neighborly. And the art of being neighborly is knowing how to listen, to share actual experiences, hearsay tales, and sometimes outright lies if they entertain. The whole idea is to share something that holds the attention—whether it raises the hackles on the back of the neck or inspires the slowest kid in the neighborhood to make something of himself.

Porch-sitting and visiting meant being together in memory—with familiar sights and sounds and feelings. They recall graduation time, Decoration Day, Fourth of July, and shivarees—those unpredictable celebrations following weddings. To "set a spell" simply meant being willing to have a say in things and to have a listen when someone else wanted to talk. It meant caring a lot without saying it in so many words.

* * * *

The laurels in our lives come so seldom, and we tend to measure life from one high point to another without realizing how important the time between really is. It moves so rapidly, and we discount it as nothing unless we have reached some spectacular new era and have passed ten other people on the way.

Sensitivity to the moment can be the greatest joy. Savoring an hour of doing nothing but listening, finding time to look at the stars and see a sunset. Time to feel really well for no other reason than knowing the wonder of being in this place at this time. It is wonderful to be normal and uncomplicated and unruffled, if only for an hour. And those hours are more numerous than we know. They balance out other times of excitement and intense feeling.

* * * *

How strange that we sometimes speak sharply to those we love—because we love them. And all of us have used anger to keep from crying.

We seem to go to such extremes to accomplish the necessary—or is it to protect what we dare not show for the moment.

The protection is not always for ourselves. When we're too sympathetic it simply urges more and more tears. To a point tears can be cleansing, but when they go on and on they destroy some of the strength needed for other things.

Anger has its gentle qualities, too. It serves to straighten the backbone, ours or someone else's, in times when it would be dangerous to cry. It acts like a brisk wind to blow away frustration and set things in order. Out of control, anger is madness and ignorance—but in tenderness it can be emotion that masks love.

*   *   *   *

God's greatest gift to man, as a human being, is man's will—his will to survive, his strength of purpose, his absolute determination to stretch beyond all barriers.

When man makes up his mind to reach an impossible goal, his chances for doing it are doubled and doubled again. His risk of failing falls far below what it started out to be, so that all power is thrown on the side of doing the impossible.

We can never underestimate the power of a determined will. We can never underrate the power to make a way where there is no way. When we begin to realize that the will to do something is born with us, we recognize the extraordinary gifts that we can learn to use in the right way.

*   *   *   *

There is something about looking up at the stars that gives new perspective—particularly after a storm when the haze has been washed away. Somehow, seeing that unlimited space helps to minimize a bit of worry.

To see things in their true perspective or relative importance becomes difficult when a problem exists. It can get to be the tail that wags the dog—a small portion ruling a whole life.

But when we put things in their right relationship we can look up and ask ourselves in all honesty, "Is this thing I am worrying about really my whole existence?" If it is a job, there's another one. If it is another person, we are also persons with equal importance. When we react with hope and refuse to look down, we have already taken the first step toward better things.

*   *   *   *

When we were children everything seemed magic . . . there were events and newness and turning points we could hardly believe . . . but now we are grown, and the light that revealed so much to us at that early age seems to be dimmer . . . and we look for it less.

It is true that much has happened since we were children. More threatening times have been invented, and we are aware of what is going on in all parts of the world. But time was when people were fighting Indians . . . and their fears were as great as ours in the things we face . . . and here I am, an Indian, writing to you to not be afraid . . . but to trust that these things, too, will be tamed and will come to be a part of life . . . in the most ordinary ways and in the best ways . . . for the One Spirit still reigns with supreme security.

*   *   *   *

Words are tools, weapons, good and bad medicine, and very beautiful when used lovingly.

Nothing has been used and misused so often or handled so loosely, and nothing can save the day so much as a good word.

There is power in a word. Whether we read it or speak it or hear it, we command and are commanded by using that power.

How often children are drained of self-confidence, and good feelings are totally destroyed by unthinking words. How many sick people are made sicker because of the way we discuss their condition—even though they seem to be unconscious (or semiconscious). How many relationships have been shattered and how much prosperity has been dissolved by poor-mouthing.

We have the power on the tip of our tongues to speak the word for good. But until we listen to ourselves and how we speak, we seldom guess how down we are in our use of words.

Those who freely speak their minds at every turn usually forget their own words and expect everyone else to do the same. But many people say little and remember a long time—as Bruyère remarked, we seldom repent of speaking little but very often of speaking too much.

Spouting words is merely an act of flushing out a little mind. Only the very callous or very ignorant believe in saying all that enters their thought. And apologies for saying too many of the wrong things are small comfort.

* * * *

You really make my day in those dark times when you say something to change the whole pattern of my thinking. It is so quieting then, when it seems every noise is magnified, to feel your presence near.

You comfort me most when I am distraught to tears, and you say very little but stand close by—allowing me to regain my dignity.

I think I am happiest when I hear your deep laughter. It is so contagious, and the gloom scatters with its very sound.

It is good to know in all the deep emotional ties that survive the ages, you are, among many things, my dearest.

And it is wonderful to hear you speak well of others. There are so many who do not—and that's a shame, for most of what we see is merely a reflection of ourselves. What we grasp in other people we most likely find in ourselves.

But your intrepid manner steps forward, and doors open and you go through, taking me with you so that I am not afraid. Because of your assurance we are all able to believe we can make it—and believing is the thing.

Such love surpasses many obstacles, and because of it there is new hope. Life has its abrupt stops and starts, but you have given me so much to go on, so much to look toward, that I cannot help but know that all things follow in sequence. When we plant good seeds we reap good harvests—so yours will certainly be abundant.

*   *   *   *

One reason we have trouble handling present difficulties is that we keep recalling other times when we didn't do well. Now seems a lot like then—and our track record is more vivid than our ability to see a way out. Even if we can't remember clearly, someone else will remind us that the same thing could happen again.

But this time we are different persons, with more experience and less need to believe in failure. What have we got to lose? When there is a chance to prove ourselves, to prove that we can overcome the meanest situations, we have everything to gain if we will just quit listening to prophecies of doom and gloom and project ourselves into a whole new atmosphere—one that is vibrant and strong and charged with the electricity of success.

* * * *

There are abrasive personalities that would grind down the patience of time itself. It takes a very special grace to bear with and be in accord with someone like that—and sometimes I am that person. We all hate to admit it, but there are times when we can be aggravation itself. We should be grateful to those who are patient with us.

On the other hand, we might try a little patience when someone else is having a bad time—even when it seems most of their times are bad. We all get caught in that trap—that pity-me-a-little-and-maybe-you-won't-be-so-angry syndrome. But we have to admit that it is all give and take—never all one way or all another, but a two-way thoroughfare that requires mutual respect so as not to clash with each other for the right-of-way.

* * * *

It is a common failing to stand so close to our families, our work, and our friends that we cannot see them in their own right—but only as an extension of ourselves.

Families frequently find themselves happier and more close-knit when they aren't so clannish.

We do not always appreciate individual members of the family until we or they leave home and we can no longer see them so conveniently or so often. They often become more dear when there is a little time and space between us.

For clear-cut appreciation we have to stand away from anything to get a better perspective. Family and friends are so important to so much of who we are that we have to leave some time and space and privacy to achieve a true feeling of togetherness and freedom.

*　*　*　*

Just as a youngster knows everything is all right when there is singing in the house, so everyone of us listens for signs of love and security and happiness we can depend on.

Sounds of happiness are sounds of security. Maybe happiness and security mean the same thing in many ways. Hardly anything sounds happier than children laughing and playing—or the muted voices of contented people in conversation. That very ordinariness gives a certain feeling of security and belief that love and communication are still possible.

We can't ever start making happiness dependent on what someone else does or says—that invites disappointment. Not that their thoughts and feelings are not important. They do greatly affect us. But happiness is apart from that.

It is an intimate thing, born with one's own being, and it lives there to support the outer feelings in times of despair and times when the height of feeling is heady.

Happiness is something we are, something within us that exists regardless of cicumstances. It is an inner private wellspring flowing quietly and at times hardly noticeable.

At other times, happiness bubbles over as though some deeper level of consciousness has revealed a reason for celebrating and, working like yeast kept warm, rises to new heights.

We search for signs of happiness and listen for its sounds, and all the time it has been in the place we never thought to look—within.

* * * *

She was one of those people who had carried a grudge so long she had forgotten what it was for . . . but it was as good as an iron gate so tightly chained that even the path leading to it was forbidden ground.

The gate was her brooding and furrowed face that fought with or without words, and it bowed her back and weighed down her spirit, requiring her to keep a constant vigil for fear someone might forget her purpose and walk past that pent-up fury.

But no one else remembered. Everyone thought of her as a grumpy old woman who wanted to be left alone, but not so alone that she had no one to notice her anger.

In only seconds she could have forgiven . . . she could have turned loose of her grudges, and it would have opened the gate. The pain would have left, and a new freedom would have helped her soar.

* * * *

Can we have a more basic need than the need to be comforted? The need for the most basic things becomes snarled with substitutes we teach ourselves to live with, things which never have substance or give us strength in any form. We are still simple creatures under the complex outer layer of pretense and disguise which we hope is our protection.

What can be more basic than warmth, water, fresh air, and quiet—touching the earth, standing in the sunlight, feeling the soft rain, tasting food when we are really hungry and not just tuned to a dinner bell. What teaches us more than the sound of music—even a voice off-key, if the song is genuinely from the inner person who sings? We cannot trade our spirits for emptiness that looks good—it must be good. Otherwise, we chase the wind—and where does it go?

TWO

AT THE BREAKING POINT— OR THE TURNING POINT?

They that wait upon the Lord shall renew their strength; they shall mount up with wings as eagles; they shall run, and not be weary; and they shall walk, and not faint.
—ISAIAH 40:31—

TWO

I so often think of you on cold winter evenings and remember how we struggled against the wind . . . wind that was cold and often unbearable and impossible to hide from . . . and it was not just nature's north winds but life's blizzards that made us wonder if there was a warm place or even hope. But we stood together in our friendship and vowed there was and that we would find it.

And at times I'm sure we still wonder if winds ever subside . . . if there are ever times when there is not a struggle of one kind or another . . . and we feel gratitude for having survived the onslaught of too much responsibility . . . and can give hope and courage to those who follow . . . for answers do come, prayers are answered, love remains, and excitement and happy expectancy still flourish . . . where we do not give up and we do not despair in the face of winter or discontent.

*   *   *   *

There are times when a reasoning mind is the last thing we need. An idea is as delicate as a butterfly caught in a blast of cold air—it struggles to survive in a reasoning mind.

We think we are being sensible when we tell ourselves it is wiser and safer to stand still rather than chancing failure. But there is no such thing as standing still. We either go forward or we go down.

Chances to grow come to us every day, but we reject them as figments of our imagination. But the imagination is our hope—if we don't talk it away or reason it away. What seemed to be totally our idea can suddenly be someone else's, developed, used, and celebrated—because we reasoned rather than worked.

There is a time to be reasonable, but there is also a time to be creative—in a positive way.

* * * *

We are creatures of habit in need of variety. When our spirits sag it is usually because we have been following the same routes, at the same time, to do the same things over and over again.

We need solitude in which to think and plan and analyze life in general. But we also need to hear voices, see new places, hear good music, and have the opportunity to communicate with other people. It sparks us to be more alive, and it revives our mental outlook.

There can always be too much of a good thing—silence, solitude, hilarity, even compromise. We all have a list of things that are just marvelous, to a point. But what we really need is a variety of emotions and activities. We enjoy being aware of what we can live and grow with, to get away from it all at times, and then to come back again.

* * * *

Spring is that time of year when nature produces its young—those fragile beginnings of new life. And few things are as fragile as a baby chicken—yet, it was born with the instinct to peck its way out of an egg at the right time.

The first few efforts to break the shell are not strong. But with each attempt the baby chicken gains the strength it needs to break through a tough wall and eventually stand on its feet.

We were not born with the instinct to succeed, but we were born with freedom of choice, the ability to think about whether we want to succeed. We may get trapped inside a hard shell of disbelief, a place where all our senses are tuned to what we cannot do. Then we wait for the strength to help us, but we realize the strength comes with the doing.

We have to make a start—begin pecking away at believing there is something better than being inside a hard shell. And when that first crack of light hits us, nothing can stop us from freeing ourselves. Nothing can stop us from standing on our feet and doing what God intended us to do.

*   *   *   *

We take ordinary events of life for granted until we discover the changes that have crept in almost unnoticed.

Those daily, homely tasks and circumstances seem so tedious and so unimportant until something crowds them out—and suddenly we know there would be a lot less peace without those familiar well-trodden paths.

When life gets chaotic, we can always think about Whittier's favorite subjects—the common things he so often wrote about—dew and sunshine, raindrops and silence. Focusing on them makes us realize how many ordinary things have something uncommonly beautiful about them.

When we can appreciate a wonderful ordinary day in

which we can be wonderfully ordinary—then we are truly aware. And when we are aware, we can cope with change.

* * * *

Some humorous soul has said that the one thing money can't buy is poverty. On the contrary, it certainly can.

It does not take money to be the richest person in town. Anyone who has survived an ordeal, where merely to exist is important, that person knows what it is to be rich. Richness is life viewed through the heart and mind—and for such a person poverty does not exist.

Prosperity is many things. Simply being well in body and mind and spirit comes at the top of the list. Seeing the changes of season, touching the faces of those we love, breathing fresh air, and knowing what it is to be cool in summer, or to be warm and contented in winter—that is well-being of the first order.

Just thinking about such prosperity is enough to make us turn off the self-pity, the acid tongue, the sarcasm and cynicism. When we want to be really rich, we can love someone—and if we are loved in return, that's becoming super-rich.

* * * *

We all have the capacity to be many things—good or bad. We probably have dominant traits, some with more good, others with more bad.

The quantity of either doesn't really matter. What's important is what we do with these traits, which part we cultivate, which we develop into the major part of our lives.

All of us have known people who made a career out of

being grossly negative, even though they may have fine opportunities. And then there are those who take one good thing and make it the chief aim in their lives—the important factor.

Whatever happens to us is the result of what we dwell on continually. We are the engineers, the builders, the directors. None of us is destined to fail—unless we decide to.

* * * *

It is those little steps that get us where we're going. One by one they count—like drops of water grooving the stone. Great strides impress us, but we seldom make them. In the smaller, daily steps we relive the race of the hare and the tortoise when winning requires faithful steadiness.

The feeling that we are not getting anywhere nags—calling our attention to the importance of keeping on. But the goal is achieved by the blending of time, effort, and, most of all, the belief in what we're working toward. When the goal is worth plugging for every little step of the way, we suddenly find we have covered a giant distance.

* * * *

There are ways of finding out what to do when we reach the point of not knowing where to turn. We have all been up against that stone wall with nowhere to go and no one to tell us what to do. But there is always a way—not necessarily to get out of some responsibility, but to change within ourselves so that we can scale the wall and find ourselves in greener pastures.

There is a method by which we can see ourselves and

our predicament objectively to help us to understand what otherwise might not come to us. We can sit quietly and project our thinking into the future to the point of seeing ourselves past this present time. Then we look back and see those people involved and all the conditions surrounding the situation as though it had already happened. Thus we can gain early hindsight. It is a matter of putting ourselves mentally in our own future shoes, seeing what should be done, and then doing it.

*   *   *   *

Every day is an invitation to us to live as well and as happily as we can. Every day beckons us to come share all that is serene and warm and beautiful. There is a joy in making the most of every moment—giving it our best because we feel the worth of that invitation to be at peace.

Every day we too issue invitations. Through our acts, our words, our thoughts, we ask for what we get. "Come make a fool of me." "Come gossip with me." "Come and argue with me."

We can short-circuit life by the invitations we send. We will always be at home to the painful guests we are inviting—all the unwanted situations we think about, dread, talk about. Until we finally wake up and then decide to change our guest list.

*   *   *   *

Some feeling of depression is quite normal. But when depression stays with us too long, we may need a helping hand to overcome it.

All of us have met circumstances and challenges that

have put us down. We have known depths when life has been difficult—but that is not the real depression.

Real depression is a smothering low that allows no breathers—never any time to come up for air, no chance to see things in a different light. It is an invisible foot that holds us down in the darkness—way down.

Nutrition, or the lack of it, plays a large part in our ups and downs. What we feed our bodies goes hand in hand with what we take into our minds. Since mind, body, and spirit work together as a whole, we cannot ignore any part of ourselves and expect to get a good performance.

We must be balanced in what we eat, in what we think, and in what we believe. And there's nothing wrong in asking for help in any of these areas—it's a sign of wisdom to do so. The rewards of asking are well worth the effort.

* * * *

Complaining is perpetual, constant recreation for those of all ages who want to talk about their difficulties but not do anything about them.

After all, what would they do without their complaints? What sort of conversation would be even halfway interesting without some difficult problem to discuss?

Any thinker knows we all have plenty to complain about. But the time comes to stop complaining and start correcting. If we aren't quite to the point of making a change in our circumstances, then there's always work to be done on ourselves.

In order to stop complaining there are many things to consider. The first is that nothing is impossible. Another is that there is a time to do something and a time to wait—and we can recognize which time confronts us only by clearing our minds of the problem and making room for solutions.

Once change begins it often comes in multiples—ranging from the easily handled small changes, to the stress of massive change. In the latter everything in our lives seems to be taking off in all directions, and it is hard to get things in order when our attention is scattered.

There is a calm center to everything. Sometimes it seems to be only the size of a pinhead, but if even that exists it can become the seed for something much larger and much better.

In the beginning, we have to know a place of calm exists—even when we can't see it. And we have to know it is within us. It is a matter of relaxing for a moment to let the calmness happen, to let it do its work.

Changes for good often come in multiples, too. As soon as the tide turns and something good breaks for us, other good things follow. That is a good enough reason to cultivate solutions instead of problems.

*   *   *   *

Echoes of many things resound faintly within each of us—voices, sounds, thoughts. Only a few ring clear, like vibrant chimes in a clock, from many seasons past.

Such persistent flashes of memory call us back—demanding we recall details—some of them best forgotten.

Why do we hear the echoes? Perhaps to clarify our feelings, to help us be more objective about the present moment. Or perhaps to force us to see the pattern of our lives so that we can correct or delete or simply be grateful.

Like the well-fed dog turning primitive at the sight of a bone, we sometimes pick up on our own instincts and react before we think. But as long as our reaction is contained within, and we understand what is happening, there is not so much danger of making others pay for what we hear in our own echoes.

* * * *

Somewhere along the way it is not uncommon for us to feel life is passing us by—that we are not getting much out of what we're doing.

It is easy to feel short-changed, as though some unseen something is hiding the key to a full life. So much of the time we find ourselves waiting in the wings for our cue to go on stage—and no one calls us.

But life does call. If we don't hear it, it is because we have not been listening. When the call doesn't sound as we think it should, we ignore the sound. Our notions of what something should be overshadow what it is, blocking out the good with everything else.

Action is the real key—however small and silent that action is. We first move with thought and feeling and understanding, the only true support for outward action. Then from such a strong base we can move with the power to be what we want to be—to find our full potential.

Our lives travel in many cycles. While some are closing others are opening. Unless we are aware, we may wonder why changes come so suddenly—or why we remain in one place without evidence of any change.

The very sensitive person can usually tell when a cycle is nearly completed and a new one is on the horizon.

Scientists have not yet determined what sets a

particular cycle in motion, but anyone who has ever experienced that feeling of change knows that cycles do exist.

Everything from dogbite to divorce has been charted and found to follow a pattern. But it is also true in the individual world that individual choices and intelligent behavior are still possible for us. We need not be at the mercy of some predetermined pattern.

No matter where we are in a cycle, it is still our responsibility to make it a good place—to be loving, open, and aware of our thoughts and feelings and careful with our words.

* * * *

Most of us like to hear familiar songs, feel familiar surroundings, see familiar faces, and follow our old and tried routines. We are creatures of habit, and we don't want anyone tampering with our well-known paths.

Because we feel the way we do about daily habits, it is hard for us to give up something we need to give up. But there is a time to everything—a time for everyone—and we cannot hold onto something past the point of common sense.

There's good in change even when it is hard to let go of something that has been an important part of our lives. Change forces us to step past the persons we used to be—or even life as it once was—and that takes courage unequaled in other times and in other situations.

It's easy to say we are not strong enough and to question the need for change—but anything that does not change will stand still. And anything that stands still stagnates and decays.

Our ability to find a new life, a new way of seeing and

doing, does not come all at once full-blown. It grows minute by minute as we take the first small steps. A firm decision to take new steps will open new doors—and from there the excitement grows.

* * * *

It takes so little to be contented—a minute away from harrassment of any kind, someone's smile or happy whistle, the knowledge that all is well with someone we love—these are the simple remedies that heal our deepest hurts.

We are not hard to please when we are content within ourselves. But when we start blowing everything out of proportion—when reason no longer exists, then we make ourselves sick. We don't always believe we have a choice, but a little quiet shifting of priorities, a little firm decision-making will show us many choices. Some of them are so deep they require thought and prayer and meditation—others are so simple that we need only to stand still and see them work.

* * * *

Nothing can ever be pure glamour—there is a gritty side to everything.

The most precious gem must be cut and polished and put in the right setting before it can be truly beautiful. In its original state it was all there—but hidden, and so comes the work to free it from its matrix, and let the hidden beauty show.

It isn't what we see on the outside that makes anyone or anything a beauty—it is the glow through to the surface, the many polished facets that catch the light.

There is always more of that work to be done, a constant need for refining and simplifying.

It's never enough to think how something looks, but how it really is—whether its quality is lasting and whether it enhances everything around it.

*　　*　　*　　*

No one is so destined to lose that he cannot turn the tide for himself if he wants to change. Losing is a choice we make like any other choice.

We are greatly influenced by our beliefs about ourselves, whether or not we are supposed to win or lose. If we think the world is against us, that is an excuse to stop trying. We may not even be aware that we need an excuse to fail—but in reality we give ourselves permission for whatever we do.

Winning is not a bad thing, and believing we can win is a very good thing. But any accomplishment brings a test we must face within ourselves. Do we really want the responsibility of being self-reliant or is sympathy so important to us that it is worth the price of losing or failure? It is all a matter of choice—a very, very personal choice.

Some of the best times of our lives are those spur-of-the-moment successes that we catch and carry lightly—as though we've done it a thousand times before.

It doesn't make any difference how minute the success is. Some of the smallest things lead on to larger victories we wouldn't have believed possible.

But there is something special about having all our senses tracking together. It doesn't happen every day, and when it does we know it and sense the ease with which we do something quite well.

So much of who and what we are is deadly serious. We plan everything down to the last detail and wait anxiously to see if our efforts merit attention—we may even pray a little.

And then on a moment's notice something enjoyable happens and we didn't plan it—we were simply there and ready to seize the opportunity.

* * * *

Never quit when things really get rough. Bear down and throw energy into every action, because the rough places prove what we are made of—not to others but to ourselves.

We prove that we have what it takes to hold the road when everything in the world would run us off.

Fear of not coming up to some suggested level can draw us off the right road. It is so much easier to quit than it is to keep going. It's so much easier to believe in someone else's strength than in our own.

We are supposed to be challenged, but the winning decision goes to the one who doesn't scare easily—the one who doesn't take a defeatist's attitude and roll over for every would-be challenger.

* * * *

When autumn begins to touch the trees it is a little sad—at first. All those lush green leaves must change, and somehow it seems autumn will change us too—and maybe it does a little, and that's not bad. It means moving, living, thinking on a different level—finding new potential to overcome old problems where once it seemed impossible.

We need a change of season to drop our old thoughts.

Colorful as they may be, we cannot keep them. If we did there would not be room for new ones, and nature teaches us that we must put off the old and put on the new. At the right time and in the right way—if we give our consent to growing and developing—we shall bloom as we were always intended.

* * * *

Only after complete dependency on other people can we really know how wonderful it is to help ourselves. It allows us to understand why some people become hostile when they have no choice but to lean on someone for everything they need.

Freedom and strength to do for oneself are a must for a whole spirit. There is appreciation for help only when it is given of free will and is not something that comes through absolute necessity. Contentment is real when there is freedom to give and take without thought of a debt too large to ever pay off. Self-reliance and happiness go hand in hand.

* * * *

Something we don't often consider when we are in the middle of a hassle is what we would feel like if we were not in it.

We find it difficult to project ourselves outside the wall of controversy that is surrounding us. We become so spellbound with the wall that all else is lost to our vision.

Vision is one of our most important pieces of equipment. With it we can see ourselves functioning effectively, we can imagine the ideal situation, and we can plan to focus on the positive way to the ideal rather than on what is wrong.

We are bound to meet some opposition. We cannot drive our car a block without having to go around something. But with our vision on where we're going, we do eventually get there.

The very personal side of us has difficulty focusing that far in advance. We get too involved with right now—but with a little practice we can see beyond that stone wall.

* * * *

There are a great many things that seem set forever in one direction—but change is subtle. Just as the sunset shifts and blends before our eyes without our sensing any change, so does life form and reform.

Sometimes we wait for years for a perfect set of circumstances to force us off dead center. When we don't find the perfect combination, and don't move, we assume nothing is happening, and sometimes panic sets in. And that is where we make our mistake.

There is no reason to wait for situations before we change our way of living—not when we can think and imagine and change our consciousness of what is important. Life is changing every minute. It must or it cannot continue. But we can be in charge, using the circumstances at hand to the best advantage—like the sunset blending and changing and changing again, until we ourselves make a beautiful combination.

We remind ourselves that sometimes history repeats itself so we can't expect too much of anything good. We have always known those who look back to yesterday and even before that. They think they would like to see change, but something hidden holds it back—holds it completely still.

It gets to be a daily duty to count the things that go wrong—one more thing, one more thing just like we expected, just like we knew it would be. It is a self-punishing promise come true.

It is a matter of looking past the mud on the windshield. As inconvenient as the mud is, it is not the important thing, but rather the road ahead.

*   *   *   *

If we were to take one concept to guide us through the day, it should be Divine Order.

Just saying "Divine Order" a few times will throw mental switches to open the way for orderly thinking and orderly acting. Without that order we run headlong into clutter.

Order has been called power, grace, good judgment, sanity of mind, health of body, peace in the city, security of the state. Shakespeare pointed out that we cannot keep any kind of outward order when there is disorder in the mind.

We see evidence of disorder in people's thinking, in the results of self-indulgence and the complications of being in unnatural circumstances. The effects are devastating.

To overcome disorder takes continual monitoring of what we think about and whether it is to our benefit. It is a lot like weeding a garden—the sooner we see the weed and pull it out the sooner the garden is free to produce good food.

Let us speak the word for ourselves, decreeing order until it is ours—in anticipation saying we are in order until order is secured.

*   *   *   *

The philosopher William James wrote in his *Will to Believe*, "These, then, are my last words to you: Be not afraid of life. Believe that life is worth living and your belief will help create the fact."

We are not at the mercy of predictions and doomers who would scare us with their ideas that life is no longer worth what it once was. Regardless of what seems to be absolute, only God is absolute.

And so it pays to believe in the goodness of life. It pays to rise above anything and anyone who would draw us away from our belief that we can do something about problems that face us.

We are intricate, marvelous combinations of mental, spiritual, and physical elements that work together beautifully when we support them with our good and positive beliefs.

THREE

NOW, PUT YOUR MIND AT EASE

*"Peace! Be still!" And the wind
ceased, and there was a great calm.*
—MARK 4:39—

THREE

Peace of mind is a jewel looked for in the worst of times and in the best of times. It is the feeling we get when we turn away from a busy highway to a secluded spot along a shady lane.

Peace of mind is suppertime when the sunset gilds every window and a quiet contentment makes man and nature akin. It is that cold drink of well water, that comfortable pillow, the shaft of sunlight that touches the spirit.

It is all the little things that make a difference, the valentine, the gentleness, the sleepy midnight song of the mockingbird—or a spring thaw.

But most of all, it is having something ring true in a time when it is hard to believe in anything. It's knowing that things are going to work out, that in the face of every denial, life is worth living.

*   *   *   *

Being alone is quite different from being lonely. Loneliness is never communicating, never blending, never feeling anything deeper than surface emotions.

No one wants to be entirely alone. Living is so much better when it is shared—even when there is tension. But to be able to spend some time alone without need of entertainment or companionship is the mark of awareness in a higher and more intelligent life.

We need each other. We need to be together to spark the vitality and energy that make living so enjoyable. But we also need some time alone—time that is not made up of loneliness, but of refreshment and renewal.

* * * *

The sounds time makes—little imperceptible sounds as quiet as our own breathing—the ticking of the clock, the cardinal's call, the rivulets of rainfall singing through the drains.

We must be very quiet to hear those sounds—and other sounds, voices, songs, thoughts—many of them memories but still so vivid.

To become still enough to catch the muted sounds will also slow the heartbeat, lower the blood pressure, order the thoughts, and make everything more livable, more workable, and eventually more enjoyable.

* * * *

We are very much aware that weariness comes more from confusion and frustration than from working hard. When we are doing something we really enjoy we blend with it to the point of forgetting to quit when we are supposed to. There is a sort of harmony and rhythm that doesn't wear us down when we're happy in our work. But we feel the pressure when there is a lot of friction.

So many people force themselves to stay with work because it offers security in place of happiness. All of us must do what we are equipped to do. But while we're about it, there is no reason not to educate ourselves for something we really love doing.

Working at something that makes us happy makes us healthy, too. There is no way to segregate a part of our lives and not have it affect the whole person. We are each a very specialized unit with no limitations—except those we impose on ourselves.

* * * *

There are hidden recesses of our minds, and we have no way of knowing all that is stored there in countless memories. But now and then we get a hint of it.

Yesterday's incident made us angry or deeply sad. We could probably have handled what happened, but it was the final straw added to all those other straws we do not recall. It was the one that marked the limits to our patience and brought on an unexpected reaction.

As the universe itself is being constantly created—so are we. We are new persons in a new day that deserves new thought—and then yesterday, and all yesterdays, lose their hold on our memories.

* * * *

If you are a winner you probably do not think a lot about it. You have been too busy working toward beloved goals, short-range and long-range. You feel pretty much ordinary folk going through ordinary routines and hoping to be in the right place at the right time for a big break.

You sometimes get as tired and disillusioned as any person. You have bills to pay, problems to solve, and a little extra help from somewhere would be a welcome surprise.

That help is not far away—it is within you. You have to beat back reason when it tries to tell you you don't have what it takes—because you do have what it takes. You have inner vision, that ability to make a picture in your mind of how you look when you are happy, healthy, and prosperous. It is a picture to heighten your awareness of the Divine potential within you—a blueprint that must precede the actual fact. If we want a rose, we don't plant a weed seed—we plant a rose, and that is what you're planting in your vision.

*   *   *   *

Our best memories may also have some degree of hurt in them, and the saddest memories may have some bit of joy.

The little things that seemed insignificant at the time are suddenly important—and things that once over-powered us have simply slipped away to nothing.

We recall a lot of times we wish we could forget—but memory is sometimes a safeguard, the burned fingers that warn us against the heat. And there can be a healing in remembering—like a fresh breeze that blows away sorrow and leaves whatever is beautiful to cherish.

We should remember wisely—it is an exercise in balance. Nothing in the past, however bad or good, should be permitted to dwarf the present.

It is so easy to recall the hours we spent as children along some sparkling stream—and there were more sparkling streams then—it's easy to remember every detail. The way sound carried up the river, how the fishing was, and how fish tasted fresh from the river and fried in an old tin skillet over an open fire.

There were violets blooming along the bank and so much poison ivy to look out for. The oars dipping in warm water sent waterbugs skidding across the surface and a crawdad into his hole in the mud—and going backward at that.

Most of our childhood memories are of small things—things our own size, but we can remember the people who shared those times, and it could make us sad—but not for long. The present time has its loveliness, too.

* * * *

It seems that some time or other I have stood here before and thought these thoughts and felt these feelings . . . and it was not yesterday . . . for I would remember yesterday . . . and I would know why I feel puzzled that I am learning something I already know.

The questioning goes on and on about who I am and where I am going . . . a very old question for a person who knows others better than he knows himself.

There is no doubt that we do not understand all we know. We are the hidden needle in a haystack that slips away in many directions, for the inner-space of us is as limitless as the cloudless sky that goes on forever, and while we waste time picking and pecking at everyone else, we could be discovering a little of who we are.

Is it true that there are no more wildernesses and no more frontiers? Don't listen to foolish talk. The greatest ones of all have barely been searched . . . our inner self and our connection with the Infinite.

* * * *

If you were a creative child, or if you have had one, you know what it's like to have an imaginary playmate. It was not necessarily a person. Sometimes it was a fuzzy animal that lived under the house—a fuzzy animal that talked and knew a good deal more than any ordinary fuzzy animal.

What seems to be child's amusing play actually adds dimension and richness, not only to childhood but to later life. Imagination helps us to have a good vision of who we are and what we are capable of being.

It may seem we no longer have those vivid imaginations working for us—but we do. We don't often realize how we use our imaginations to downgrade life—we see ourselves struggling against impossible odds and falling short of what we want to be.

We are complex combinations of many things—some are contradictory to our God-given vision, but when we can recapture the simplicity of childhood with the ability to envision only God, we will experience more of it.

* * * *

Timing is so important, and it is amazing how little attention we pay to it. Fools rush in—and haven't we all been foolish? Haven't we ignored the intuitive feelings that there is a time and a season for everything and insisted now is the time—even though the tide is running in the wrong direction?

The idea always precedes the actual event—we have to see it in our mind's eye long before it can actually exist.

We have to prepare ourselves, sometimes without realizing it—and sometimes having to make a conscious and concerted effort to accomplish even the smallest thing.

Emerson said that life is good only when it is magical and musical—with perfect timing and consent. There really is such time—but we have to be ready to flow with it.

* * * *

In all our wanderings through life, we develop faith in a lot of things—some of which prove themselves unworthy of such devotion. And then doubt creeps in.

Doubt is our most constant companion. It has the power to take the zip out of much we thought would always be at a high point. But doubt can also serve as a clearinghouse.

Sometimes when we feel especially threatened it pays to think through all sides of a question—as long as we don't let fear monopolize our thinking.

If our fears and worries do nothing more than strengthen our faith in our all-loving Father-God, we will have made excellent use of our time. To develop a faith that is not a narrow, immature prayer for trouble to stay away, but a joyful shaft of light leaving no shadows and penetrating the deepest corners of our minds—that faith brings peace for this life, the gentlest and most healing of all our faculties.

*   *   *   *

There are so many things I wish for you . . . that you are always strong and able to fulfill your dreams . . . and see the flowers and touch the sky and feel the earth beneath your feet.

I wish that you could always be charged with energy and purpose . . . to feel the peace that passes understanding and meet the eyes of those you love.

I wish for you a mile of road where no one has discarded a paper cup or bottle . . . a free-flowing stream not jammed by junk . . . an open field where deer feed without fear . . . and people who want to rise above themselves and all the conditions that suggest they cannot.

I want all good for you . . . peace and happiness, health and order . . . and a belief in yourself to follow your star!

* * * *

If there is anything we have plenty of right now, it's negative opinions. The normal pastime seems to be to talk down the best efforts of anyone with the courage to try for health or prosperity or anything beyond our own comprehension.

If we stop to listen, we can sense the fear that causes such opinions. So many sound as though they are authorities when they talk and talk—but haven't we heard it before?

All our lives we react to rumors and hints and suggestions—some seem so logical. Yet, if we kept a list of opinions and predictions—our own and other people's—and checked them out, we would find as many wrong as right.

No two situations are exactly the same. We cannot rely wholly on history nor should we fear it. What has passed has passed, and we hope the weaknesses we've known have gone, too.

We may not have control over other people's opinions and how they talk away their own good, but we do have control over our own thoughts and reactions. When we determine to work more and talk a lot less, we grow and survive the mass of empty opinions.

* * * *

At some time or other, life gives us the opportunity to negotiate our freedoms—makes us aware of how unaware we were.

Sometimes we fight with fervor for a freedom that turns out to be hollow and without much meaning in the long run. Other times we gamble with everything most precious.

Like a bird in a cage with only inches of flight space, some of us are inclined to look out at the wild birds on wing and think how much we would love to spread our wings, to soar, to migrate. And yet, a bird on the wing has no protection, no loving care, and no regular feeding.

There is need for self-examination, much to consider. If there is any wisdom to be found, it may be in the realization that sometimes the very things that pin our wings also help us to faster growth—and show us how to handle our freedoms more intelligently.

* * * *

The owls call to each other early on a snowy winter evening. The blue hour comes more quickly, and nature's nighttime creatures awaken sooner.

Some move through the deep woods with easy motion—others broadcast their presence from treetop to treetop or gather in small packs to howl in high-pitched wailing.

In that almost-dark hour the silence becomes profound—suddenly there are no voices, no footsteps, not even the sound of wind moving through the branches of ancient oaks.

The time is brief from dusk to the last glow, but for those few magic moments it is almost as though time stands still.

And then the stars begin to twinkle and the voices

resume their evening songs. But for a moment we have caught what seems to be perfection.

* * * *

Sisters are lovely . . . even when they've known the depths, they can rise to the occasion and take their stand alongside someone else . . to bear the brunt of painful times . . . to reach out with comforting hands and loving words to lift us up again.

True sisters never condemn us for being late . . . never complain when we fall below the level of common sense . . . and love us even when we do something foolish. They are not miffed when we forget a special time . . . and they do not resent our times of winning.

Sisters are not always blood kin . . . what does that matter when the relationship is stronger than ancestry . . . and love transcends all the shoulds and oughts and makes us a family by choice . . . so what could be better than having a sister?

FOUR

THE SIMPLEST
REMEDIES

*Our God turned the
curse into a blessing.*
—NEHEMIAH 13:2—

FOUR

We cannot always see that we have a choice. Whether we explode or take things in our stride is a matter of choice. And life may require a little of both before we can really get down to the business of knowing what counts and doing something about it.

The simplest remedies come with our deepest needs—rest and peace of mind, good nutrition and long walks, prayer and forgiving, spells of solitude, and something to love. Keeping it simple is the difficult part.

* * * *

Many times our aches and pains are caused because we don't move around enough—neither in our minds nor in our bodies. We have to use our muscles, put them to the test on a regular basis if they are to stay healthy and move freely.

But this is so of our minds, too. We need to challenge our ability to think through a situation, to see what we *can* do with our minds.

When we start letting things slide, giving up on what we can do, we relinquish a little bit of our freedom. The freedom to be independent is a very precious gift and should be cared for as lovingly as any gem.

What others say to us may affect us, but only if we're open to their words. It is the things we say to ourselves that make the difference—things like telling ourselves we can't do something simply because it challenges us.

Every day we have to rise above something or we'll find ourselves sinking under circumstances—and who can afford to let that happen?

* * * *

Nature makes an effort to clean up behind us and to cover her own wounds. Wind gathers up a lot of trash and rain melts as much as it can, but we are really too fast for those natural forces. Tons of discarded debris leave our hands daily and land in every possible crook and cranny.

It is sad that we care so little about our surroundings, that we litter and have the idea that someone else will clean up the mess. We go through life leaving all kinds of messes for someone who cares enough to do the work of cleaning up. But there's always a day of reckoning—a time when everything balances and our turn comes. In some form or another our carelessness comes back to us. The thought is a none-too-gentle nudge to remember the next time we decide to dump on someone else.

* * * *

One of the good things about being alive is having an awareness of things visible—and also being conscious of what we can't see.

On a spring night after moonset everything is black velvet. There is a quiet awareness of life invisible as soft breezes brush the face and the fragrance of flowers drifts on the evening air.

Sometimes even nature has difficulty sleeping on those nights, and there's a sudden burst of song from the mockingbird. It's a serenade to life—a tension-reliever for deep inner relaxation.

In such awareness there is no need to worry about the trials that come with daylight. We learn to take our ease when we can—being grateful for a bed and the chance to rest, even when we can't seem to sleep.

And soon, early morning sunlight filters softly through new green leaves, and breezes like gentle fingers play across the grass.

Early morning is the time to live in the present—to enjoy the sound of an eager titmouse in search of food, to listen to the squirrel barking at an invader in its territory, and to hear the mother cardinal coaxing her young to try their wings.

It is time for us to come out, too—to emerge from the cocoon we've built around ourselves and take a look at a whole new world.

* * * *

Sitting at the edge of the pond in early morning as shafts of sunlight cut through the mist, the looking and listening makes one realize there's beauty even in ugliness. Consider the unmusical, but very pleasant, sound of frogs croaking. Look at the ungainly white heron standing there with its long crooked neck and skinny legs—yet it is graceful and beautiful as it circles the pond and lights on the limb of dead oak. The oak is as stark as a piece of modern sculpture whose difference makes it beautiful.

It's how we look at something—how it affects us that makes it ugly or beautiful. We must appreciate the emotion it inspires and understand its importance in the plan of things. If beauty is in the eye of the beholder, then the eye must be in the heart.

* * * *

Living alongside other people can affect us in some very strange ways—even when we don't know those persons.

It's a lot like sitting in one's car at a traffic light and suddenly becoming aware of the overpowering smell of idling cars, a few vibrating rattles, and some unusual bumps and thumps. We wonder whether some of those troubling sounds and smells might be coming from our own car—and there's a period of intense listening to detect a problem. But as the light changes and cars draw farther and farther apart, most of the sounds disappear.

We are like that when we listen to other people's symptoms. We listen to our own heartbeat, take our own pulse, and hunt for things that might match the symptoms others say they have. But as soon as something else demands our time and attention we forget a lot of what we were afraid was happening to us.

It is wisdom to pull away from the constant sound of trouble and recenter ourselves on something creative and constructive.

* * * *

All of us need time for our wounds to heal. And even then we must be protective of the scars because often our hurts are still near the surface.

We may think we've passed the point of remembering, but then something happens to bring the pain out again.

It takes time and then more time to erase the hurt of

such memories. Even the tiniest traces can balloon to tremendous dimensions.

To watch for those times, be conscious of them, and deal with the hurts and pains within ourselves will eventually dissolve them completely. There may be times when the memories surface again just so we can clarify our feelings about them. But when we can meet them face to face without giving them life through renewing the hurts, we can be rid of their influence forever.

The important thing is to be patient with ourselves. And that's the hardest part.

* * * *

It's wonderful to have some happy reason to get up in the morning, to be enthusiastic about the hours to come. That sort of attitude usually requires some little incentive, some feeling that this is a special time—a very special time to be alive.

Enthusiasm is the major part of doing anything well. Some feel glad just to be alive, and others feel life is a day-to-day endurance test. One person has confronted the worst of everything and feels the miracle of survival—another has never really had much trouble and is bored with his own breath.

Do we have to be threatened before we can enjoy? Or do we just need to be alive within ourselves, to know the meaning of gratitude and opportunity—to be willing to grow?

A simple change of attitude makes all the difference. It helps us know that being victor or victim lies within our own power. What we believe we must experience, we will.

* * * *

We are peppered all winter with suggestions of flu, all summer with suggestions of rashes—a variety of diseases for all seasons. We are told we should check for this or that and be prepared for all kinds of difficulty. That sort of philosophy suggests that we are vulnerable to a lot of things—but we may not have to deal with them at all.

We have within us a natural immunity to most everything that fails to get our attention. There are times when we foolishly leave ourselves open to problems— usually those stemming from stress. But to believe we must fall prey to every passing germ is even more foolish.

Every day is a new day when we can reject the idea of how weak we are.

*   *   *   *

Long walks are as good for the soul as for the body . . . and we have walked a lot together, you and I . . . watching the birds circle overhead, hearing the early morning chimes, and feeling the reverence that comes unbidden.

We have walked out a lot of problems . . . trudging along thinking and communicating without words . . . finding companionship without touching, except in our minds.

We have seen gorgeous sunsets . . . watched the farmers plow their fields . . . we've fallen for the tricks of the killdeer, trying to lead us away from its nest with that old broken wing ploy . . . the flirtatious tanager has caught our eye, and we have stopped to listen to the mockingbird's medley.

But the best part of all is the walk back home . . .

knowing we have walked out our troubling thoughts . . .
shared something beautiful and inspirational . . . and
walked contentment in.

* * * *

Suppertime should be one of the nicest times of the day,
bringing us together in thought and tradition—even
when one person dines alone.

Most people are sharing a meal at this time. It should
be a warm and friendly hour when the events of the day
are shared—with no complaining and no distractions
from the pleasant atmosphere.

Everyone should learn at an early age how important it
is to gather together—and be taught that the dining table
is not a grievance board. Good feelings and happy
attitudes enhance the taste of food and closeness of
relationships.

Good digestion is a result of good humor, of love and
laughter. They all work together to bring us into
harmony with each other.

When we sit down to eat together with expectation
and joy, we can work together in the same way. We
know we can even disagree and still be friends,
especially if we agree to keep this time free of criticism.

* * * *

There is a warm feeling of sharing when people with a
common problem stand together. They may support
each other silently, not having to know all the details, but
simply acknowledging that there is an emotional bond.

The strength of minds and prayers united for one
purpose can produce miraculous results, and events are
moved in such a way that we cannot question the power.

Standing together has nothing to do with the old saying that misery loves company, but in the company of others who are determined to find the right answers there is great strength.

It is comforting to know we're not alone—and we'll never be alone as long as we can reach out to each other in warm support and understanding.

* * * *

The danger of our increasing years is not in growing old but in losing our interest in living.

Vitality doesn't wane so much as interest wanes— interest in feeling well, looking well, acting well.

We give in to situations that wouldn't bother us at all if we had not conditioned ourselves to believe it is time to feel this way. We tend to monitor our pulse and our age.

But it is time to stop telling ourselves how the years have caught up with us. We are personally responsible for how we react to the years and events of our lives. If we have been rigid thinkers, we will have rigid minds and bodies. If we have been petty and tiresome, our bodies will be, too, and we're not going to get any better unless we change our attitudes. Other people will not enjoy being with us. To put it quite simply, age magnifies what we have been all along.

Our present state is not something that arrives with age, but it has kept pace with us from the beginning. We are not without remedy, and we can change—by seeing ourselves as we really are and changing our habits. That kind of change knows no limits from age or number of years—but comes from self-appraisal and the willing-ness to do something about what we see.

There are times when we ask why. Why is life handing me this particular thing to deal with? Have I done something to bring it about, or is it simply a twist of fate that time may still turn in another direction?

The questions are mingled with doubts and faith at the same time. But we are not alone.

We arrive at certain points in our lives when trusting is the only help—not necessarily trusting in other people or in things, but in a Higher Power that is unexplainable.

The more we try to explain it, the more we lessen the majesty; and yet blind faith is not the answer. Blind faith is accepting something because it is easier, because it fulfills a sense of need for doing something methodical—even though it changes nothing.

Trust is a deep inner knowing that springs to the surface in love and patience and joy. It does not judge or condemn—but it does heal. It produces seeming miracles.

* * * *

Hunches are those little providential promptings that come to us at odd moments.

Usually they come when our hands are busy at some familiar task, leaving the mind free to wander lightly over all those things that matter so much.

Then suddenly, like a bolt out of the blue, there is a thought too strong to ignore, so strong that it stops all other thoughts until we do something about it.

A hunch is worth following to see if it means anything. It is one of those little gifts of knowing, an assurance that we do have some sort of radar working for us.

Grandeur is very near our dust, Emerson said. God is so near us that when something whispers we are capable of doing great good—something within us knows we can. But to accomplish the good, to follow through on a hunch, requires of us more listening than talking. If we talk too soon, telling others about it, we deplete the gift.

* * * *

Love and hate are so far from each other around the wheel of emotions that they frequently stand back to back.

We often find it easier to hate someone than to love that person. Hate gives us something to pit ourselves against, to push around so that we can feel the strength it gives—while love is so melting.

If only we could stay angry and hate something long enough to change it—if we really want to change it.

So often we rely on the intensity of the feeling hate inspires to hold us up. A sudden release might leave us aimless, like a dog off a leash—we wouldn't know what to do without that emotion to direct us.

We seldom bother to hate people or things that mean nothing to us. Hate left alone does not grow but gradually dissolves. When we keep it well fed it separates us from our better selves—while love unites and heals the deepest wounds and worst fears.

* * * *

To forgive ourselves for not being superhuman is almost superhuman.

Not to be able to see everything from beginning to end is frustrating—not to know if this thing we're doing is right and if the outcome will be to our liking.

Risks are a fact of life for anyone doing anything. Those not willing to go out on a limb for something they believe in will stagnate. It takes a certain boldness to strike out and do something different—especially when someone points out that it has been tried before.

Nothing ever remains quite the same—for which we can be very grateful. But there simply comes a time when we have to follow new guidelines and think new thoughts and do new things. It doesn't take a superhuman, but it does take a worker, a believer—an inner ear that hears more than is being said.

Sometimes we stand so close to something dear that we can't see how dear it really is.

Our lack of awareness robs us of what we assume is ours forever because we take for granted something beautiful—and someone else doesn't.

We have many eyes—but most of them are closed or glazed over. We have the eyes of the mind that perceive far more than our physical eyes will ever see.

The eyes of our hearing will detect not only sound, but feeling and atmosphere and the music of the spheres.

We have the eyes of touch that not only feel, but see the gentleness or firmness and the depths and heights of emotion.

We are never blind except when we close ourselves off to seeing with our senses the greatness of gentle things.

And then we see that being superhuman is not the answer at all—the answer is being superaware of the spiritual gifts that lie deep within our God-given natures.

*   *   *   *

Speak often of softer things—of flaming redbuds and shimmering dogwoods, of the singing finches, the flowering grass, the drifting clouds.

Remember how weary you grow of never hearing

anything that builds your spirit or feeds your soul—but only things that tell you about all the ills of the race and the forgetfulness of those you love.

Know when raindrops fall it is to nourish the deepest roots, to sprout the seeds, and sweeten the grapes. And when the sun does break through, it will shine clearest through the unclouded windows of your spirit.

Remember to talk of gentler things, of good plans, good hopes, good crops, good life—or be quiet, refusing to talk at all.

*   *   *   *

How nice to sit with you over a cup of coffee and not have to say anything. . . . How good that you do not try to entertain me or pass this quiet time with a lot of idle chatter.

How restful that you do not care what the neighbors are doing—nor would you tell me if they did hold your interest briefly.

Even when I am provoked with you, you never hold a grudge—but look only to our resumed friendship . . . waiting patiently for me to make a move to show I'm feeling better.

And I appreciate your lack of criticism and your apparent forgetfulness when I have forgotten to show you my love . . . and I, too, will try to be more patient when you prefer to dig in the flower bed . . . or chase a squirrel or bark at the neighbor's cat!

*   *   *   *

What seems to be a mess of trouble often proves to be a blessing in disguise—if we can only hang onto our common sense and sanity long enough to recognize it.

Most of us wonder what possible good could come from some situations . . . and so far as human reason is concerned there seems to be no possible good, but human reason has wiped out more than a few miracles . . . when a little steadfast faith and determination have brought about miracles.

The universe is full of magical things—events and turning points and newnesses we can hardly believe, but they exist just the same—and they exist for us . . . when we catch hold of a vision of what is right and hold fast to our faith in a loving, all-providing Father.

*   *   *   *

Thoreau said that men will lie on their backs talking about the fall of man and never make an effort to get up.

No one person can take all the blame for what is going on in our world. We're all in it together, even though we may not feel we have taken an actual hand in affairs. If we condone it and allow it to happen, we are partly responsible.

There's a time to speak and a time to keep silent. But there's also a time to work, a time to clean our own houses, a time to stop the foolishness we're so often dragged into.

Whether it has to do with our country, our way of life, or one's very personal life, it's up to each of us to reclaim and demand that living be kept in its most responsible form.

*   *   *   *

Life has a certain likeness to running from fire—if you turn back to collect your old grudges and pick up the hates, you're going to get singed.

There is no way to get to any place worthwhile until we learn to leave behind the smallnesses of the past. No matter how deserved these things were and how much pain has gone into collecting them, we cannot be free and clear until we stop looking back to drag the past in with us.

Common sense can be the ultimate difference between life and the other alternative. We have to know that nothing is as important as this moment and the next—and it is not intelligent to jeopardize this time with yesterday's memories.

*   *   *   *

Sometimes we have to be dreamers and be sensible at the same time—know how to fly and also walk calmly, be lifted above questioning and still remain serene.

Circumstances change—life changes. It changes for the better, and the elation is a little intoxicating. It is the first taste of sweets, the feeling of freedom—and the need to talk about it.

Talking is the biggest drain on the spirit. Tell no man—relish the knowledge of something untold, the feeling of highest privacy.

We can talk away our good by sharing too much that isn't ready to be shared. It depletes the reserve of serenity and well-being to talk foolishly, to project too much of ourselves for no good reason.

Silence is more golden than we have realized—for in silence much is born, much is saved, and much bears good fruit.

FIVE

BALANCING THE LOAD

So shall you know that I am
the Lord your God, who dwell in
my holy mountain.
—JOEL 3:17—

FIVE

Everyday living is a lot like lifting weights. When the strength of one thing is equal to the weight of another there is balance. But when too much weight is added at one point, balance is lost, and we can drop the whole load from sheer exhaustion.

To accomplish anything, we have to have order. To be orderly, we have to know what is important and what to let go—but this is where the difficulty lies. We do not always know that until we have everything up in the air, and we may have to put everything down until we learn.

We are not strangers to pressure. We even tend to think there is something wrong if we're not beating ourselves to pieces trying to balance a load. With order we are not so bound, not so apt to tilt—and what we can do, we do better.

But the days go by, and the challenges to carry a bigger load are with us. We wonder how in the world we will ever get through. And we do get through—not all at once, but little by little, step by step.

It's that little bit at a time—doing the best we can on a minute-to-minute basis. We cannot lift a load the first time we try. But in isolated instances even that has happened. Love and devotion and overwhelming need have given such instant and powerful strength to seemingly puny people to lift impossible loads.

Those instances should show us the reserve of strength that can be poured into us at such moments—

and make us aware that we have access to it in lesser amounts if we will make demands on it.

To know even a little of the potent strength at the point of a powerful need should let us know we don't have to climb a hazardous mountain all at once—but little by little, breath by breath, prayer by prayer.

* * * *

Pushmataha, chief of the Choctaws, understood our weaknesses so well that he advised, "Never be elevated above measure by success . . . nor delighted with the sweets of peace to suffer insults."

He knew how willing we are to give in to abuse for fear of having no peace at all—peace at any price so familiar to so many.

And he knew how a little success can do away with common sense—how it can remove the stops that keep us from going overboard.

It is important to find a stable attitude somewhere between those extremes where we sometimes find ourselves. A century has passed since Pushmataha gave his sage advice. He was suggesting we cultivate inner peace and look for success within ourselves before we get carried away with our surroundings.

The good life is an inside job—peace with ourselves.

* * * *

When an old car goes down the road at an odd angle we know it is out of alignment. We also know if something isn't done to correct the alignment, the tires will wear out.

The same thing happens to us. There is so much emphasis on illnesses and remedies and verdicts of the possible and impossible, we just can't help but realize how important it is to be well-adjusted and well-aligned.

We are as capable of sending and receiving as any radio equipment—we are constantly broadcasting what we think and feel and taking in what others are telling us. We are susceptible to suggestion, open to what we hear and see, to the point of taking on difficulties that are not really ours.

So much information is poured upon us daily in an effort to sell us something or to ask us for contributions to further a cause, that we are afraid—afraid of being the victim. But there is an immunity to fear and hostility and worry, and it is built by serenity and prayer. It is the most natural cure, the best protection, the only really sure thing in our lives.

* * * *

One of the pitfalls in having things go wrong is beginning to believe we can't do anything right.

When we don't know the truth about ourselves we believe in failures and impossibilities. When we have trained ourselves to fall, we fall. The very first sign of opposition makes us think failure.

Just as any of us can be accident-prone, we can become failure-prone. Daily thought includes what we can't do more than what we can. Even our fears of contagious diseases, or having something we've heard about, weighs on our minds.

But what have we inherited of difficulty? We have been pelted with the idea that everything bad lurks everywhere to drag us down. Subtle advertising for profit has made us victims of our own beliefs. We begin to believe it takes a lot of money to protect ourselves—a lot of running scared until research produces something to stand between us and trouble.

We lean heavily on anything that will help us get through the next few minutes—though the golden key is already in our possession to open new doors to new lives. That gold key is to change our way of thinking.

If we have inherited anything from those who have gone before us, it's apt to be fear. Because they played it out before our eyes we believe it. But have we questioned—were they, too, victimized by their predecessors? The belief is a chain that must be broken.

It doesn't make any difference how dear the persons were, or how much they loved us, or even how good their intentions were, if they conditioned us to believe we are victims, we have to break that spell. We do not have to be victims unless we give in to the idea.

It takes a determined and strong individual to go out on his own and break with a tradition of fear. It means changing our minds—not once, but many times. We have to correct our course again and again until old habits and old ways of believing are dissolved and new and better ones are reset.

Mankind has many gods to whom sacrifices are made—but there is One that asks no more than we lay down our false beliefs about ourselves and become powerful individuals.

* * * *

The magic hour, it is said, comes at midnight—the turning over of one day into the next. Midnight is the time of long moonlit shadows, or the velvety black in the dark of the moon.

It can be a quiet uninterrupted time, or it can be the

hub of the evening—according to where you are. But it is another of those definite lines we cross and recognize as special.

Why is the midnight hour any different from any other hour of the day or night? We have many magic hours in our lives. They come at odd times to remind us of what has passed or what lies ahead.

For many, hours go by with little notice. For others, an anniversary, a birthday, a something special becomes a magic hour.

The most majestic hour of all is when we quietly, without fanfare and without making any kind of stir, step past a struggle that's no longer a part of us and start all over again—now that's magic.

* * * *

A thought is a small thing—yet, one inspires another until a mental image is formed. From that mental image life's blueprints are drawn—and from those blueprints worlds are built.

Hope is a little thing. One tiny glimmer of hope can lift us out of the deepest pit of darkness. One whisper of courage helps us know that as long as there's a modicum of hope, there's an excellent chance.

A wish is a small thing. Like a little prayer it climbs the steps to an idea and gives us hope to make our wishes come true.

From small things great things are formed. In little beginnings are all the seeds of great events.

* * * *

When we first learn we have the same God-given ability to laugh as we do to cry, we've taken a giant step.

Even though it seems we are sensitive to pain—more so than to being overjoyed—we are frequently saved by something humorous to enliven our dark thought.

Good deep laughter springs forth with a spontaneity to lift the saddest heart and to mend a broken one. The very sound of laughter sends a message to everyone that life is still workable and still worth refining and savoring. It is then that we dare to hope.

We all know we can't meet all life's circumstances laughing hilariously. But we also know there is a time to laugh and a time to cry—and sometimes the line between the two is mighty thin. But to laugh, even during a time of sadness, means regained strength and peace of mind.

* * * *

Every kind of crafty plan in the world has been devised to help us fool ourselves. It works for a while. We follow a formula and lose weight, smoke less, drink less, and succeed to a point—and then the enthusiasm and energy begin to wane and we are back looking for a new plan.

We don't particularly like to think about how long it took us to form a habit. Some of them come more easily than others, and some we never meant to let form at all. But hardly any of us consider what will become chronic until we can no longer resist something that isn't good for us.

All of us want to change, but the long-range effort to remove a habit requires so much effort—especially when we want to see quick results. We have to change our thinking rather than devise ways to trick ourselves. Training the subconscious to reject what we do not need and replacing it with what we do want is worth everything we put in it. It means allowing our wiser part to direct our senses—those sharp senses that so quickly react to outside stimuli.

*   *   *   *

Lethargy is a form of self-hypnosis. It holds us inert like a slumbering bear in the middle of winter. It is not because our bodies want to sleep but that our minds do. When that feeling is present we give in to apathy until we are beyond expression.

Lethargic drowsiness is a dull, vacant feeling that dissolves only when we put our minds to work on something interesting. More food, more drink, more rest make no difference. And sitting and leaning get heavier and heavier—but taking an interest changes all that. When we find something the mind and hands can become absorbed in, it arouses our interest and the mental chains fall away.

Usually such dullness comes because we have too many things to do and none of them interests us. If we had a clean slate, new ideas would rush in, and we would get busy. It's when we feel we can't really enjoy anything and leave our jobs undone that we let lethargy have its field day.

If we can approach our work by seeing it through someone else's eyes we might see new ways of doing it—and find it interesting enough to do well. It means pretending—seeing our work as others might see it, and finding we want to do it.

*   *   *   *

Nothing is worth the bitterness that so easily takes over when an injustice is done. It affects us in so many ways, causing illness and discomfort—and even accidents.

When we're distressed about something, everything takes on a sour, uneasy atmosphere. And when we're exhausted, things can look so much bigger and so much worse than they really may be. But the effects are the same, and bitterness is apt to be the result.

Frequently, we let a problem slide rather than handling it quickly. At first, that seems the easiest way; but as time passes, the unfairness of it begins to eat away at our peace of mind and before long there is no peace.

We have two ways to save ourselves. One is to get in there and set the record straight—the other is to forgive and forget. We are a lot better at forgiving than we are in forgetting, and as long as we can remember, the chances of being bitter are great. If we lose our tempers and say too much, that hurts us, too.

There is a point of control—that inner mountain where we go to observe everything in its right perspective. It means rising above our emotions to where we have a cool and balanced approach, like a game of mental chess.

At this high point we can accept our own responsibility for any part of what may be right or wrong. But we can also see the other side from all angles, and without the emotional interference we will be able to make decisions and settle differences we couldn't have handled earlier. It's worth climbing that mountain to avoid standing in a rut for the rest of our lives.

*   *   *   *

We all discover at some time or other that it's painful to love . . . that caring about something, about some place or about someone is a very great joy . . . but it opens us to hurt to . . . by making us vulnerable, easy to get to, easy to touch . . . and hard-pressed to disguise our emotions.

Some bit of us wants desperately to hide what we feel . . . for fear that it will be taken the wrong way . . . but even more than that for fear we are revealing more than we are willing to have anyone know . . . we need that reserve of self so not to deplete all that we are . . . so not to give away that part of us which generates life . . . that keeps us able to love and feel deeply. But for all the pain that goes with caring—we wouldn't lose it for anything.

*   *   *   *

Some of us can't bear being alone and others of us are woodshedders—going off alone to think and ponder why things are the way they are.

We really need to be a little of both—to have a chance to talk but also a chance to listen to what someone else is thinking. We need each other to balance the load of living, to compare ideas, and to learn about our own strengths and weaknesses.

We all need something to keep us moving and healthy—a need or a longing to get somewhere beyond what seems possible at the moment.

Most of us have a rut we lovingly think of as a groove. It's a comfortable place—maybe too comfortable for our own good. We can settle in a little bit too easily and withdraw from contacts that might not always be pleasant but that keep us on our toes.

We have a right to be alone when we need it. It is one of our most valued rights. But we do our best work and think our best thoughts when we've shared an hour with a friend.

*   *   *   *

We can never discount the need for friends—we need every precious one of them. But there are those special ones that come along so rarely we can't help but recognize the difference between them and "ordinary" friends.

Special friends are with us in spirit—no matter where we are. Their loyalty supports us when we need it, and their silence is never a reason for doubt—never a reaon to question whether we are still friends.

They make us secure in the knowledge that no matter how many others fail us we can count on them. Without words or the need for their actual presence, they are, in Emerson's words, "fit for serene days and graceful gifts and country rambles, but also for rough roads and hard fare."

To have such friends is necessary to us—and to be one is every bit as important.

SIX

THE WASTED
YEARS

*I will restore to you
the years which the swarming
locust has eaten.*
—JOEL 2:25—

SIX

The nautilus is a seashell, beautifully formed like an unfolding spiral. And it is probable that a tiny membrane serves as a sail to help it float on the sea's surface.

Each year the nautilus works to build a new chamber and moves into it, leaving behind the old one sealed off and forgotten.

Instinct, the wisdom of nature, directs the nautilus to grow—to leave behind what it no longer needs. That's some distance from our own thinking and practice—we drag it all with us. We keep an accounting of grudges and hurts, and a few happy times we use to compare with our feelings of today.

It is hard for the present to compete with what we recall of yesterday, and what we expect of tomorrow. Today is just a pause in our flight, we think. But the present is so important, so good, so patiently waiting for us to wake up and grow without the burden of the past.

We worry so about the wasted years and the lost time. If only we had done things differently, had chosen a different route, or could have seen things in a different light. If we had only taken some thought, we might be in a better position now.

We can even regret being happy or contented now—because we didn't start sooner. The contrast is so startling, and we wish we had known how to be happy in those lost years.

Summed up, it's like saying, if we had known then

what we know now. But we didn't. It wasn't the time to know. Whole lives are given over to regret and resentment. And still further time is given to those wasted years.

When we stop regretting we can recall Joel's promise that the years the locusts have eaten will be restored to us. It is then we stop remembering with regret and start living the joy of today.

Mark Twain said in his youth he could remember anything—whether it happened or not. We're not so different. We recall many good old days that couldn't have been that good.

Memory gets out of perspective. We park by past events that were supposed to be grand instead of passing on for even better times.

If we could have recorded all our words and thoughts and events on an hourly basis, we would find as many good ones here and now as we ever had in the past. When we stop living in the present we stop growing. To stop growing is the last thing we can afford. And we can't afford to let the past dwarf the present any more than we can refuse to look toward tomorrow.

* * * *

Living has its difficult moments when anything worthwhile seems far away, but in times like those it pays to remember other times when we have doubted our ability to cope. But we did, and life went on with an order we never expected.

There are those places we walk through that tax our strengths and test our will to rise above our own doubts and those of others, but those places are not permanent, nor can they take away the best part of what we know and feel.

The fact that we have known peace makes us know we will have it again—in greater portions, in sweeter times, in more lasting ways, because we are who we are, children of spirit, we bloom, like the flowers—in perfect sequence.

*   *   *   *

Confusion causes more weariness than all the hard work we ever do—and it lowers our resistance to anything that challenges our overall good health.

English divine Frederick William Robertson said that true rest is not inactivity but harmony. We have to level out, find a natural place, and handle every situation with more ease.

Robertson added, "It is not refusing the struggle but conquering it—not resting from duty but finding rest in it."

Harmony is breathing evenly and easily wherever we find ourselves. It is refusing to listen to the voices of dissension. It is standing still and letting everything find its proper level, its proper place.

Harmony is pacing ourselves to an inner clock that never gets out of timing. We have more going for us than we know. We can learn harmony when we become quiet enough to hear guidance.

*   *   *   *

Envy is such a weak emotion, yet it is destructive and can turn a perfectly intelligent human being into a totally useless victim of self.

Envy is poisoned imagination of no quality except to

detract from good. Its very existence strips us of loyalty to anyone or anything, and the more we try to hide it the more evident it is.

Eleanor Roosevelt said it most clearly, "No one can make you feel inferior without your consent."

Inferiority breeds envy and does it with our full cooperation.

*   *   *   *

Language is something we rely on for much of our understanding. We are lost in areas where we are not understood, and even more where we do not understand. It is not something limited to a particular tongue but to a manner of speech, a way of expressing what we think and believe.

To feel secure, we cling to words that do not reveal who we really are. We hide behind slang and build defenses with useless conversation and the latest catchy phrases. We are measured by what we say—from piety to profanity. It scares us to be measured by anything, but language is the window through which the real of us is clearly seen. It is the language of the eyes, the set of the head, the turn of the body. It is the openness or rigidity of our attitudes.

We scare people away from us by our language. We want them to like us, but too often, what we say holds them at an arm's length and makes them uneasy. Gentleness is universal. With it, all language is beautiful. Without it, we can expect more division and less respect.

*   *   *   *

There may come a time when we will wish we had made a different decision from the one we feel compelled to make at this moment. But don't we have to depend on whatever wisdom and good judgment we have right now?

Remembering wrong decisions may color our efforts to make a good one now. We have to know that during the time we have had since we made those other decisions we have progressed a little.

We may never become so well organized mentally that we do not make mistakes—since it's only those who are not doing anything at all who never make an error.

Indecision plays havoc with our emotions. We waver between doing something and doing nothing. One minute there's a clearcut answer and the next only chaos.

A line of action can be mapped out that seems feasible, and then it suddenly seems filled with pitfalls. It usually happens when we're dealing with other lives—pondering the intrinsic nature of other personalities.

There's nothing wrong with questioning. It often saves us a lot of grief. Instability is frequently a sign that things are not settled—nor can they be as long as indecisive emotions cloud the mind and spirit.

How often such weaknesses steal our common sense and run wild with the unreasonableness of false guilt, bringing us to the brink of being destructive. And then, having reached that point, a quiet calm settles over us, and truth seeps in. We know we've never been alone, and we are not being condemned for our decisions—but only for our fears. There is no fear when prayer releases our hold on all other things. There are no wrong decisions when we are in the presence of our Counselor—that Holy Mountain where everything good is not only possible but probable.

*   *   *   *

All along a summertime lane there are wild flowers, deep purple and yellow and lilac—sometimes even pink, which is unusual in the heat of summer. Huge coils of hay have been placed in rows, and smaller bales have been hauled away to storage, leaving meadows of new green from summer rains.

It is a welcome relief to walk these paths and see nature taking her special ways with wild animals and birds. Young quail walk along the same path, lifting themselves on tiptoe by flapping their wings—the exuberance of the young and untried.

We close ourselves in a mental cocoon of worry and forget to look at the tranquility, forget to soak up the serenity and peacefulness of these basic things of nature. It's all there. We simply have to attune ourselves—to sense, even in memory, those times that fed our spirits, and allow them to do it again.

* * * *

Fear of the unknown has made us all question our sanity and question ourselves as to what we're doing here.

But in the process of growing we must go through some strange places and think some unusual thoughts.

As frightened as we are of so many things, we can still remember Emerson's words, "What a new face courage puts on everything!"

We rally because we begin to know we have what it takes, and the fight to win comes back with double force.

It is natural to feel some strangeness, but if we never move out of our narrow existence and learn to reach for our full potential—how will we know what we can do?

With a little courage—a result of sincere prayer—we can do, and will do, the impossible!

Should you find yourself in indecision, in darkness, don't let it worry you. It simply means the dawn is coming.

There are degrees of darkness, different severities, but to the one standing in the dark, dark is dark and sufficient to its time.

Persons outside that shadow cannot understand what all the fuss is about and have little compassion. But one who has been there knows and remembers—and can say with great gentleness that the light is coming.

The part others often fail to tell is that the night will pass more quickly when we allow it to be dark. In our confusion we believe that we are caught in the longest night—but even that can't hold back the dawn.

But we get very tired of waiting for that dawn. We wait for answers that seem suspended somewhere. And some well-meaning soul insists we smile—but smiles are on the surface and not always real.

We're now at the bottom of the wheel, and the wheel always turns if we keep working at it. It may get bogged down and tempers may rise, but there will come a morning when visions of how things can be are more clear and inviting. Then we are glad we didn't quit—that we followed through one more time and the answers came. They came with the dawn, because we didn't lose our faith.

* * * *

English critic Henry Hazlitt called it a great art to be silent in conversation—to communicate through one's presence and add to the conversation without need of words.

Such conversations with our Father-God must surely be more effective than the many words so easily and habitually repeated. Communication is so much more than just talking. Much of the time it is silence that speaks most eloquently.

Silence allows everyone to take responsibility for what is being said—and it gives us a chance to leave unsaid all those things that later we wish we hadn't said.

Comfortable little quiet spells in conversation are as rare as jewels. But conversation is like painting a picture—often what we leave out makes it interesting.

* * * *

We all have things that make us nervous, even emotional, to the point of distraction. We forget how subtle feeings are, how they suggest to us the complete run of negative events.

We are such complex combinations of muscle, nerve, and emotion that we seldom realize how a stiff neck may actually be someone who's a pain in the neck—or that an itching allergy may be something or someone getting under our skin.

We try to bear up under the load, telling ourselves how dumb we are to let something bother us. But our frustration has to come out somewhere. If we control what we do and what we say—what better place to express it than through the body?

Life is too dear for us to live always under pressure at the expense of our mental and physical health. But there's help in recognizing the problem, and there is satisfaction in doing something about it.

By everything we say and do we program our days and our weeks and our lives. If we expect everything to be hellish life will certainly accommodate us. If we believe living is supposed to be good and happy—it will be, but it will not become that way quickly. We believe more slowly in the good things than in the bad.

We program ourselves either to step over trouble, ignoring it, or to get down and wallow in it. Most trouble is accepted because it brings a sympathy and attention that comfort us.

We set ourselves up to live a certain way—to be either happy or unhappy, tolerant or intolerant, easy to have around or difficult, making everyone wish we would go away.

There is help in knowing we are not always in the wrong. The law of averages tells us everyone has something to contribute, and some of it has to be good. It is a personal decision we need to consider when everything is bothering us.

*   *   *   *

How often we walk the halls of memory, and how devastating it can be to us. And yet, there is also a healing in recalling hurt. It is a fresh breeze that blows away the sorrow and leaves the beautiful part to cherish.

The loveliest memories in all the world have some degree of pain. And the saddest recollections have some bit of joy. The little things that never seemed to amount to much are suddenly important, and something that once overpowered us slips away to nothing.

It is practical to remember some times past. When we revisit certain occasions and situations it takes the sting out and allows wisdom to come in.

*   *   *   *

Early on summer mornings before the sun has penetrated the dense shade around the pond, there is a quiet hour. It is a moment of solitude before all the hours of rushing to get something done.

A few wispy clouds are reflected in the glassy surface until a turtle pokes its head through to distort the calm and disturb the image of yellow wild flowers fringing the water's edge.

This is a place of contentment—this knowing that no matter how fast I must run later, I will recall this time. This moment is made for me.

The locusts sing and the dragonflies are on mosquito patrol—cattle are feeding along a far slope where summer rains have greened the hills, and I am gaining strength.

This is one of those dear times when nothing detracts, and everything adds a feeling of well-being—one that recurs when I need it, when I need it in the rush of too many things.

* * * *

I like to think of you when the leaves are all shades of chrysanthemums . . . and sunlight is golden and falls lightly through the haze.

I like to think of you laughing and contented with life . . . knowing you are never given a load too heavy to carry . . . knowing you are not alone . . . even when no one is in sight.

I like to think of you when all is quiet at the magic hour of midnight . . . or when the moon's light bathes everything with silver.

I like to think of you when love overcomes your fears . . . and peace permeates all your existence . . . for nothing is as pleasant or as fulfilling as being with someone who is at peace.

I just like thinking of you.

* * * *

Make this a day when nothing can get under your skin, not gossip, not pettiness, and certainly not the urge to argue.

Make this a day of relaxing past the coping state, of being so on top of difficulty that it cannot entice you to come down and deal with it.

Make this a decision day where all those things in the fallow state for such a long time are moved, handled, and completed.

Make this the sweetest day you have known in a long time. Take the opportunity to be yourself, your real self, a true friend that does not discourage or threaten or ridicule—and does not further entangle you in something that does not enhance you in any way.

This is your day to mold, to control, to make so new that tomorrow will be totally yours—and eternally yours.

* * * *

A shadow doesn't always show us what causes it. It is a silhouette or a dark outline cast by something standing in the way of light. Frequently it is quite opposite from what it appears to be.

A cluster of leaves can throw a shadow that looks like a huge snowflake—but nothing could be farther from the truth.

And so it is with chasing a shadow over someone else's reputation. What frequently appears to be a suspicious fact may not be a fact at all, but something that gives the image.

We would be lost most of the time if we had to depend on appearances. We are so intrigued with what we want to see that we actually see it—until the truth moves and the shadow does not.

* * * *

To be secure we have to have something to eat, something to wear, and some place to live—but we require more than that to be comforted.

We need to believe in something good, in someone—in ourselves. And brought down to the finest point, comfort comes from the most unusual sources—a favorite pillow, an old pair of sneakers, a quiet spot away from the crowd.

We are creatures of habit with needs that go deeper than what we work for daily. We need to be alone with ourselves—to let down and enjoy a moment when there's no pressure.

Such a recentering process rests us more in a few short minutes than hours of unconscious sleep. It is a letting go to a far deeper rest through the simplest ways, "like words of hope that dart into our souls and give us comfort."

*　　*　　*　　*

He is a little man. His hat is a bit askew as he walks slowly and thoughtfully. He pays little attention to the world about him, and sometimes in conversation his language leaves something to be desired.

Frequently he is smiled at because of his eccentricities, and that doesn't bother him. He knows where he has been and he knows where he is going—a decided improvement over most of us.

Unless you take time to know him, you would never guess that a giant of a man walks within him. His kindness, his financial aid, whatever he has is there to help him help someone else. Many have been in his debt, but he never asks for payment.

The park bench is his favorite place, and the squirrels

are his friends. He has a deep love for nature, and he, himself, has a need for kindness and attention.

He is a little man—but he is a stone we dare not cast away, for he is a diamond in the rough—a jewel in the rarest sense. Let's not pass him by without seeing him and ignore his humanness—or yours.

SEVEN

TO TOUCH
THE EARTH

*The day is thine,
the night also is thine:
thou has prepared the light
and the sun.
Thou hast set all the borders
of the earth:
thou hast made summer and winter.*
—PSALM 74:16-17—

SEVEN

Touching the earth is a lovely thing . . . a feeling of once again finding our beginnings . . . a knowing that this place where we stand, whether to walk or plant or plow . . . is something created for us, a place to stand and feel comfort spread quietly through us . . . for the pulse of the earth slows our own and tranquilizes our confusion.

Seeing the sky in all its limitless depths stirs our imaginations . . . and stretches our awareness of how much simple beauty is provided for us . . . and we can see the smallness of being bitter and know it lasts only as long as we allow it . . . but when we reach beyond the ceiling of our minds, we can be as unlimited as the sky.

As currents of air stir the fragrance of flowers . . . we may not be able to see all things, but we sense the influence and know that life is ours to enjoy as individuals . . . ours by Divine heritage.

* * * *

Is there anything with more beautiful seasons than a tree?

It stands in beauty from year to year and retains its grace and dignity. It keeps its secrets and tells nothing of passing events or the antics of people.

We can learn a lot by observing trees. A vigorous growing tree is constantly pruning itself, constantly shedding any excess.

If a tree must stand in a difficult place it sends down deep roots to grapple for a firm footing. A fresh green tree removes many toxic poisons from the atmosphere and emits clean fragrance to rest us from our heated days.

To sit beneath a tree, or to lie beneath one, is the essence of pleasure. But to see the topmost leaves no human hand has ever touched is to see a common miracle—a miracle with a message. It is telling us to get a firm footing and stand tall with our eye on the sky.

* * * *

The woodland has been a place of enchantment, a world of lacy patterns and mysterious stillness. The snow-and ice-covered limbs of the old oaks formed their own intricate patterns against the sky, and ribboned lace, white on white, extended across the frozen pond.

Only one spot in the ice is thin, where deer pawed through the ice to drink and then moved on leaving tiny hoofprints in the crunchy snow.

It is the only time of year that the cottonwoods blend with the landscape and the cardinal becomes a brilliant contrast. Nature's patterns and designs are etched in ice and in life.

We have such patterns in our own lives—cold, untouched ones, brilliant colored ones. Some are efforts to survive, and then there are the beautiful, quiet, solitary moments.

But we do not see the beauty of ourselves as we see the beauty of nature. We feel the harshness and sense the difficulty, but we view the beauty as something unrealistic, illusionary—but sometimes it is the illusion that is most real.

* * * *

Home must surely be the dearest place in all the world. It isn't where we once lived—or where we live now, but that place within the heart where perfection has built a special place called home.

Within this place are all the happy memories, all the victories, all the bright plans for happiness.

At certain times, familiar sounds and scents and even colors will open the door to this cherished place and we know a happiness, a contentment, beyond description.

It may be the homecoming sounds of country life or children playing at dusk. It may be the farmer calling his cows or the squeaking of a rusty hinge as a gate opens—and a voice that lifts our spirits, a fragrance from the ovens, a thousand and one treasured things that mean more than just the ordinary. They mean home— and the feeling is a wonderful homecoming.

* * * *

April is the color of jonquils, the fragrance of hyacinths, the dewiness of violets.

The sunlit meadows are carpeted with tiny blue flowers, and along the ravines wild strawberries are as sweet and tart as the air. It is so important to be alive now that April's here!

We forget that while the earth sleeps life is never asleep—that in a matter of hours it can become a whole new existence, a complete new set of rules.

What was once brown and somber now abounds with color, radiant color, and the very air seems the color of sunlight.

Everything in spring takes on a new aura, and only we spirit-beings must prod ourselves into action—for April is already aware of life. Life starts beneath every decaying leaf and on every limb and bush and creek bank.

It is in the moss and lichen spreading across the rocks and in the call of the quail searching for its covey. Morning haze lifts from moist fertile ground, and the plow turns up rich black sod ready for planting.

It is a time for deep breathing, for savoring this part of nature that man did not create—but that was made for him. There is a newness here that draws out our own willingness to live and to do it better.

It suggests something beyond what is seen and felt. It hints that if things haven't been going well for us—we can change them.

Only a few short weeks ago the earth was frozen and impossible to work and cultivate—now it seethes with energy and life. And in the weeks to come life will teem with breathtaking shows of beauty. But we are not apart from it—we too, can have new life.

* * * *

Underlying all the threatening circumstances that seem to confront us daily are those bits of humor to help us survive the ignorance, the uneasiness, the caustic.

We expect a little of it in humans, but nature, herself, has a substantial amount of humor built in: the rough and tumble play of puppies, the comic shuffle of the black beetle crossing the walk, and the grasshopper's idiotic springing straight up and falling down in one spot.

No doubt if nature were aware of some of our normal behavior she would see the humor in what we do. She would see how we cry over changes—even though they make everything better, how we make ourselves sick over conditions that have no value in comparison to our health.

What we most need is to be shown how we rely on anything and everything except what we have within us. If something within us will see that whimsical bit of humor, it can show us the way out of self-pity.

* * * *

When it's May in the woods, every bird is staking out its territory. The songs it sings tell not only its mate what the intentions are but all other birds as well. The tinier it is, the more challenging—so that even the bluejay in all its sassiness is no match for the chickadee or the finch.

Every piece of fluff or string or straw is eyed with jealousy and collected zealously to line the nest and prepare for the young. Here is nature with a purpose— and nothing daunts its instinctual plan to carry out that purpose.

Purpose is a strong force for winning. It even exceeds talent in human nature. And it surpasses skill, when skill isn't used to its fullest potential.

When we know within us how something will look when it is finished, we push forward with a purpose— carrying a vision so strong that nothing can stop us.

It is a winning trait to have a good steady purpose and to challenge even the big obstacles that would defy it.

* * * *

Early summer mornings are as fresh and new as the baby calf that bounds across the meadow. The mother cow looks on as anxiously as we do when our children are out of bounds and we're not sure of what they are going to do.

There's an unequaled loveliness to a summer morning. The first rays of sunlight sweep across a sea of dew-heavy wheat and dodge the low glens where darkness still hovers—and the doe and fawn cling to that filtered shadow of protection.

Moisture from the pond rises to cooler air and vaporizes into floating white clouds. The sun throws long shadows in distorted silhouettes. And there are great sweeps of wild flowers, Indian paintbrush, verbena, bright yellow cone flowers, and purple vetch like swatches of beautiful fabric thrown over the land.

Getting up early is not everyone's delight—but if one must, there are rewards. Here is an overnight miracle—everything that was tired and wilted and spent has suddenly been revived. Everything has a freshness to stir the mind.

The summer tanager's trill is clear and crisp, and the squirrels scurry in all directions in playful moods as the day prepares to unwind. From some past miracle comes a reminder from Thomas Carlyle, "This world, after all our science and sciences, is still a miracle; wonderful, inscrutable, magical and more, to whosoever will think of it."

* * * *

It's that time of year when the lakes and rivers and creeks call to us when we need rest. The drawing power in even the thought of those peaceful places is immense.

Sunny meadows and rolling moonlit prairies have their own restful charm, but water has always been more than a necessary liquid. It is the symbol of deeper meanings—as Seneca wrote, "Where a spring rises or a river flows, there should we build altars and offer sacrifices."

Spending time near water seems to unravel the messes we get ourselves into—encouraging us to relax the hold our problems have on us, and the nervousness that is a result.

Beside those meandering streams we plan to read or even work—but that seldom happens. The lake atmosphere blanks out the past and the future, and we make our sacrifices by forgetting for a little while the things we think we should be doing. We sacrifice our belief that something cannot get along without us and before long we breathe more quietly, rest more deeply, and think more accurately. Living can be in Divine Order.

*   *   *   *

Walt Whitman wrote, "I hear America singing, the varied carols I hear" . . . each singing what belongs to him or her and to none else.

America is still singing. Sometimes it is drowned out by the crying, by political promises, by growing pains, but it still sings nonetheless!

There are reasons for tears, we can't deny, but there are also reasons to celebrate freedom, to believe this is the greatest of all nations. We prove it every time we vote.

Each of us has an individual song to sing, and our need to be heard is great. There is a song of protest against ignorance and prejudice and disease. But there is also a song of joy—a joy that makes us all brothers and sisters.

It is a joy that helps to dissolve greed and selfishness so that we can sing in one harmonious voice.

This is our America!

*   *   *   *

August hayfields are dotted with sage-colored bales and flocks of birds hunting for bits of grain dropped by the mowers.

It is summer, and summer means sun-kissed faces and golden meadows, warm breezes and harvest time. It is a turning point from growth to maturity—a maturing that is still growing but in a different way.

But it is also a resting time—one of the loveliest times to sit beneath an open sky and feel hours pass without rushing off to lesser activities.

Honey-slow and warmed by the sun, this moment takes on the essence of times past when things moved with less agitation. And yet, nature doesn't stay quiet long. All the sounds are suddenly mingled with birdsong and breezes. If one sound is not harmonious, all nature stops to listen—and then gradually the drumming, humming, buzzing sounds all return. A cluster of oak leaves rustles in the breeze, a bug begins a sing-song tune, and the tree toad starts its evening rapture in a voice much out of proportion to its size.

There is genuine rest in this quiet place—not because of the quiet—but because of the harmony with which nature runs her creation.

It is now that everyone is rich in spirit—able to hold those moments of peace close without having them dissolve. We are past planting and not quite to the harvest, so it is a good time to heal, to gain strength, and to give ourselves a store of wonderful feelings to draw from when we need them later.

When we have returned to work, to the freeway, to the closed-in places, we can shut our eyes and hear the clicking of crickets, the humming of the locusts, smell the fragrance of fresh hay—and drain away the tensions.

*   *   *   *

Even before there are visible signs of autumn, there are subtle suggestions of change.

A summer laziness gives way to a new time, a new color most vividly displayed in the deep woods. There is a feeling of preparation for something different, of little hints of cooler air. There is the innate knowledge in nature that change is inevitable—and good.

This is one way nature and human nature oppose each other—one changes by instinct and the other by decision.

Even though we deny it at times, we do get tired of battling change so we give our consent. It is usually a surprise when we find change was for our good—and yet, resistance to change is constant. We are comfortable in the familiar, even when it isn't particularly good. And then something forces us out of our rut, and the beginning of something new becomes an experience we wouldn't want to miss.

*   *   *   *

Signs of autumn are appearing with every morning's sun. The vines that have slowly crept to the top of the old oaks are tinged with scarlet, and hackberries have clusters of gold leaves. The meadows are carpets of bright yellow flowers, and once in a while there is the strange song of a migrating bird.

Even though the night air is crisp and cool, it reverts to summer warmth during the day. And the harvest moon is much too bright for sound sleep—as though we need longer hours to gather in the harvest.

The squirrels are working to store pecans and acorns and are fattening themselves on hickory nuts to prepare for the long winter.

This is one of the most beautiful times of year, the blending of one season into another, with its earthy fall colors and pungent smells of smoke and damp soil turned up by the plow for winter wheat.

Up in the meadow the soft rolling slopes have turned rose-beige as the grasses ripen and lean with the wind.

Gus-dog disappears from sight into the lush undergrowth until a covey of quail explodes overhead and scatters in all directions. The deer have already begun to blend with the landscape—an innate part of their protection. Cows call to their calves for supper, and evening progresses to quiet time.

The evening star rises more quickly now. And the sunset's splendid colors blend, one into another, with liquid movement until all are folded away to make room for the moon's cool dignity.

To be a part of all this is a gift. To view the natural sequence with which nature moves her creation is a breathtaking experience—and we begin a new cycle, always a new cycle.

* * * *

The child in each of us is just as alive today as in all those Thanksgiving Days past. The road that wound through the woods and crossed the creek to Grandma's house is still there. The light dusting of snow on autumn leaves still blows in our memories. The egg-gathering for pumpkin pies and the long-drawn-out process of making mincemeat have not faded in the least.

We are children of times past, and no matter how much the ways of the world change and how sophisticated we may seem to be in our attitudes, those basic beauties are as vivid as ever.

It may be that difficult times have made us grateful for everything—but most likely it was the warmth of sharing something good. It was something called family and friends, and even a stranger if he should happen by. We may have had cold feet sometimes or were afraid often—but the real is still real, the fragrances, the aromas, the peace, the love of a special day with special people. Now, that lives forever!

* * * *

Early autumn mornings are wrapped in low-flying fog so that even the birds are cautious in their flight. Clusters of rose-colored grasses are draped in dew-laden webs— and all along the path silken remnants shimmer with the most intricate designs.

For a few hours the morning is softly hung with gossamer. Some of the webs are already in the process of being repaired where a leaf or a larger insect tore though.

But each has the mark of a special spinner—silver in the fog and invisible in the sunlight.

Surely the tartest spirit is sweetened in these hours—the walk not only makes the heart beat steadily—but lightens it as well.

* * * *

Once you've heard the sound of geese in flight, you never forget it.

That special clean call stops you wherever you are and directs your attention skyward. No matter how muffled the call sounds at first, we tune everything out until it comes in clear and spirited.

It is awesome to see geese flying in huge formations. Hundreds of them follow their leaders, turning like silver flecks in the sunlight, slipping through the night with only that special sound to announce their passing.

The sound of the geese is the sound of freedom, declaring a change of season—the clear call of the wild that progress has not affected. It tells us that things have not changed all that much—we are still a part of that beautiful nature.

* * * *

Today as I swept the last of autumn leaves from the doorstep, I thought of the happy hours we have spent sitting there through almost every season.

In spring we watched the first purple hyacinth unfurl its waxy green leaves and the first robin hop over still crusty ground.

In summer we sat there and watched the moon silhouette the pear tree and coax open the faces of the moonflowers.

In autumn you ran scrambling through piles of colored leaves in pursuit of a squirrel.

Now here we are again approaching winter, and we will share the hour of feeding the birds and clearing the walks—but most of all we will enjoy the crystal clarity of a winter evening.

I often wonder whether you are my faithful pet accepting food and time and love—or, when you wag your tail and bark, whether I'm your pet, someone for you to watch over and tease and sometimes tolerate.

* * * *

There was a time when I wanted to run from winter—until I learned to blend with it.

When I was warm on the inside and there were no

chilling fears, I could better lean into the wind, pace myself to breathe the cold air, and taste the snow without absorbing it.

The winter world has a crystalline quality that makes sound carry more clearly, scents smell more savory, and faults be more clearly viewed.

Like anything else—if one is prepared to meet it rather than cower at the thought—winter is an excellent time to be happy and alive, expecting good hours and cheerful companions.

Winter is a season made for us—a part of life we do well to make the most of and enjoy, so not to lose a moment.

* * * *

There is something about a Christmas sky when the night is clear and still, and the stars are bright enough to light the way without help from the moon.

The countryside lies quietly under such a sky . . . peaceful and serene, with only the soft hoot of a distant owl . . . even the cattle stand quietly—only on occasion stamping their feet as they move softly in the herd.

It is nature's way to soothe the land and give us peace if we can let it be—if we can tune into the silence and feel the absolute tranquility that lets go the hassle of too much activity in too short a time.

Christmas night is a special gift to each of us . . . when we can hear the distant bells and feel the utter quiet that is balm to the soul in this special hour . . . to know what it means . . . to want to include us in a new birth.

* * * *

There are not many days left in the old year, and it seems a good time to let all the old problems go out with it.

We should consider what we want to let go of now, so that when we get to that imaginary line between the old and the new times, we will have determined some direction and have some plan.

Most of the time we get nowhere because we don't know where we want to go. Often it is not doing something hard that gets us down but the indecision about it beforehand.

We drift from one year to the next, always intending to do something that gets less important with time, and finally we give up.

Giving up is not to our advantage—having a vision of what we want is to our advantage and will get rid of lethargy and laziness in short order.

The feeling of accomplishment fosters a whole new way of life filled with plans and hopes and excitement that keep us young and moving.

For every person believing there is no reason and purpose to life—there is. Wait a little while, take the next step, do the next job at hand, put aside self-pity and self-contempt, and it will turn the tide.

These are difficult times. Who can deny it? But things have a way of working out when we stop pouring hot tears of resentment on every thought and idea. Hardship has a way of being a blessing when we have a vision—the ability to see beyond what is right in front of us. Bitter thought can breed bitter circumstances, and love attracts love. Give yourself a chance, relax, and put your mind at ease.